THE WALLS OF INDIA

THE WALLS OF
INDIA

Prose by
GEORGE WOODCOCK

Paintings by
TONI ONLEY

LESTER
&ORPEN
DENNYS
PUBLISHERS

First edition

CANADIAN CATALOGUING IN PUBLICATION DATA

Woodcock, George, 1912-
    The walls of India

ISBN 0-88619-067-3 (bound). ISBN 0-88619-092-4 (pbk.)

1. India - Addresses, essays, lectures.   I. Onley,
Toni, 1928-   II. Title.

DS407.W66 1985   954   C85-099061-0

Royalties from this book are being devoted to rural
medical aid in India, through the Canada India Village
Aid Association (CIVA).

Jacket: *Tibetan chöten, Darjeeling*, Toni Onley
Paintings photographed by Robert Keziere

Design by The Dragon's Eye Press
Typeset in 11 pt Bembo by
Q Composition Inc.
Maps by Jonathan Gladstone, Geographics

Printed and bound in Canada by
McLaren Morris and Todd Limited for

Lester & Orpen Dennys Limited
78 Sullivan Street
Toronto, Canada M5T 1C1

Contents

List of Illustrations

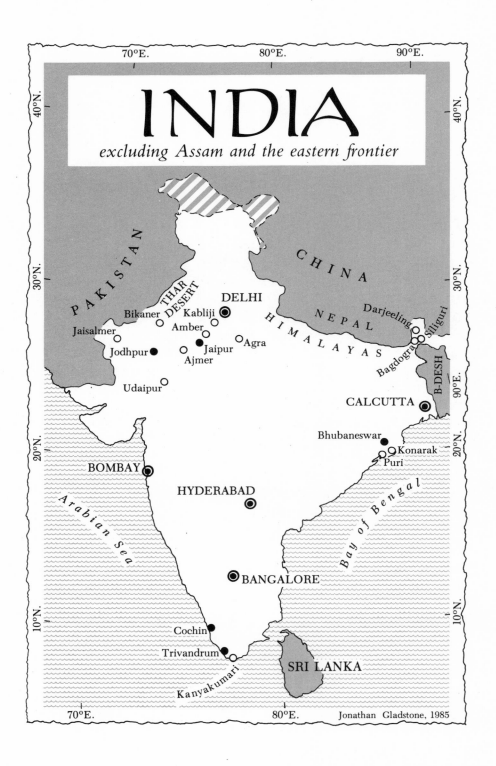

INDIA

excluding Assam and the eastern frontier

70°E. 80°E. 90°E.

40°N. 40°N.

PAKISTAN

CHINA

THAR DESERT

30°N. 30°N.

NEPAL

HIMALAYAS

DELHI

Bikaner Kabliji Darjeeling Siliguri

Jaisalmer Amber Bagdogra

Jodhpur Jaipur Agra

Ajmer

B-DESH

Udaipur 90°E.

CALCUTTA

Bhubaneswar Konarak

20°N. Puri 20°N.

BOMBAY

HYDERABAD

Arabian Sea

Bay of Bengal

BANGALORE

10°N. 10°N.

Cochin

Trivandrum

SRI LANKA

Kanyakumari

70°E. 80°E. Jonathan Gladstone, 1985

I

INTRODUCTORY

December 12–30, 1982

1. A Cycle of Ind

On December 9, 1982, we flew out of Vancouver to begin the journey from which this book has emerged. There were five of us: painter Toni Onley and his wife Yukiko, my wife Inge, myself, and our friend Tony Phillips, who would accompany us on the first stage, through the deserts and hills of Rajasthan, in the northwest of India. Tony's friend, Margo Palmer, would meet us three days later in Delhi and join us on our journey through Rajasthan.

We went by way of Tokyo and Hong Kong, and our route to Japan took us on a west-north-westerly flight up the coast of British Columbia. The intricate shoreline, rain forests plunging into deep fjords, curved like a green and blue fretwork below us, and to the starboard side, from our cruising height of thirty-thousand-odd feet, we looked east over the "sea of mountains" that is British Columbia, the ranges backing each other line by line to the Rockies, and all in the first, fresh, glittering beauty of early winter.

For Inge and me, it was our fifth journey to India. Our previous trips had been long ones, leaving few regions unvisited, and I suppose those months of experience, which in the end added up to years, had earned us the equivocal title of Old India Hands.

By the time we first went there, I had long been drawn to India, partly through a lasting admiration for Gandhi's achievements, which had helped fashion my own political attitude as an anarchist-pacifist, and partly by friendships made in 1930s London with young Indian writers, and especially with the novelist Mulk Raj Anand, who in turn had introduced me to another friend with close Asian links, George Orwell.

Various circumstances – the impossibility of travel to Asia during the war years, our move to Canada in 1949, long journeys in Latin America and Europe during the 1950s – delayed the trip to India that had long been in my mind, but by the beginning of the 1960s the idea became more urgent. I had developed a curious feeling that a missing part of myself was waiting to be recovered there, and in 1961 we boarded a P & O liner at Port Said for the classic voyage of the Raj: through the Red Sea and via Aden across the Arabian Sea to Bombay. Inge had been doubtful, half-resistant, about travelling to India, but when we looked out of our porthole across the harbour to the palm-crested island of Elephanta on that glittering autumn morning, she too recognized that we were in a wholly strange land, yet felt we had come home.

On that first journey, by train, by bus, by car, by air, by riverboat, by elephant and even by palanquin, we wandered on a vast sweep through India, from the Kashmir border to Darjeeling in the north, and southward as far as Cochin and the holy city of Madurai, leaving the country by the ferry that crossed to Ceylon (as it still was) at Adam's Bridge.

I had a commission to prepare a documentary for the CBC on the influence Gandhi's life-work still wielded thirteen years after his death, and this led us into political and social circles the ordinary traveller would have no reason to enter; Mulk Raj Anand, now back in India, introduced us to the literati; a chance encounter with Khando Yapshi, the Dalai Lama's niece, led us to the heart of the Tibetan refugee community at Dharamsala. There we gained the Dalai Lama's lasting friendship and a mission that would tie us to India for a decade and more, for it led us to found, when we got back to Canada in 1962, a Tibetan Refugee Aid Society that subsequently did a great deal toward resettling these fugitives from the high Himalayas into the Indian foothills of those mountains and the jungled hills of Mysore.

Out of the first trip I wrote a book, *Faces of India*. When I read it again recently, I was struck partly by a vividness and clarity of visual perception, which showed how intense and immediate the experience of India had been, and partly by a quality of innocence that extended from my younger self to the country I described, or perhaps vice versa. Doubtless, the last quality stemmed from my own excitement at encountering a world at once so familiar (because of all that had been written about India under the British) and so alien in almost every aspect of its life as soon as one got beyond the great cities that had been founded by foreigners. But it had also to do with the time at which we made that first journey.

India, in 1961, was still that country of immense variety which the British had nurtured by preserving the double system of rule: the directly administered territories of British India – land acquired by the

East India Company before the Indian Mutiny – and the native states, including areas as large as European countries and tiny realms smaller than most English country estates, whose rulers had the power of life and death over their subjects and usually reigned, on however small a scale, as absolute monarchs so long as they did not provoke imperial disapproval by some wholly atrocious act of cruelty or tyranny.

When India became an independent country in 1947, the native princes were unseated and their former realms incorporated into the states which made up the new country, but in 1961, a mere fourteen years later, there still survived enough of the differences they had pre-served to give India a quality of exotic diversity that it has since slowly lost. Perhaps we went at the best time, when the old tyrannies of Raj and rajas had come to an end, but the ancient local life styles that had lingered under their sway were still largely untouched by homogenizing influences.

Coming back from that and later journeys, I would tell my friends: "There's one infallible rule about travel in India. When you go to bed at night you know that next morning there'll be something new and surprising and interesting to encounter. There's never time for bore-dom." I was telling the truth about India as I saw it then, but it is not so much the truth any longer. In its ways the India of today is far less varied than the India of 1961; the daily surprise can no longer be guaranteed. To an extent this explains the different nature of this book from *Faces of India*, and even its title, *The Walls of India*. For now, as Indian life in its turn begins to suffer the creeping uniformity that has submerged the various and the eccentric in our own world, it is the enduring man-made and natural monuments, the *walls* of its ancient buildings and its vast mountain ranges, in which its special character is most strikingly preserved. But there is more to the title than that – and there are other walls; the walls of caste and the walls of language, the walls created by religion which still cause bitter and bloody conflicts, and perhaps the stoutest wall of all, that between the prosperous and the poor, that vast and seemingly irreducible mass of people at the base of Indian society, generally estimated at 300 million in number, underemployed, without land or real homes, and so destitute that many of them survive on less than a dollar a day.

The later visits to India produced more books. Out of a journey in 1963-64, which took me to other Asian lands as well, I wrote another travel narrative, *Asia, Gods and Cities*, and a history, *The Greeks in India*, that told of India's contacts with the West long before the British appeared at Surat. We spent a 1965–66 visit mostly in the turbulent little southern state of Kerala, with its ancient Christian, Jewish and Moslem communities and its bouts of agrarian communism; out of this emerged a combination of history and cultural survey I called *Kerala: A Portrait of the Malabar Coast.* And then, after our fourth journey to India in 1969–70, I wrote my fifth Indian book, *Mohandas Gandhi*, which was less a biography than a disguised dialogue with the master who had played such a crucial role in my own mental development and whose influence had led me in the beginning to his country.

I recognized that India had rejected Gandhi. Yet this very rejection had released his teaching to the world, where his defiance of militarism and of state glorification helped to shape the protest movements of the 1960s and 1970s, which in turn developed their own versions of his methods of *satyagraha*, nonviolent noncooperation. In making this recognition and in writing *Mohandas Gandhi*, I was externalizing my Indian preoccupations, seeing them on a universal scale, and in this way, liberating myself from my long fascination with India. This did not mean I had lost my feeling for the country. Far from it. I continued to read Indian books, to follow Indian news, to write on Indian events and authors, and when visitors arrived from India I welcomed them like fellow countrymen. Yet for a decade, I travelled to other places, led partly by circumstances and opportunity, partly by the feeling that a cycle of my life had ended.

2. The Web of Life

That cycles repeat themselves is a basic assumption of Indian thought. And by a strange and compelling web of circumstances, I was drawn back to India, after more than a decade of absence, in the winter of 1982–83. It was my fifth visit, and for Toni Onley, my collaborator in this book, it was his first. The threads of the web that drew us together and then drew us to India reach back to the first day of my first visit to the subcontinent, when Inge and I encountered Patwant Singh.

Patwant Singh is an Indian writer and the editor of *Design*, his country's best magazine of architecture and planning. His father was one of the Sikh contractors who, under the direction of Sir Edwin Lutyens, built the dramatic complex of rose-coloured stone buildings in the heart of New Delhi that was designed to enshrine the authority of the British Raj and is now the node of power in independent India. Through a mutual friend's letter of introduction, we met Patwant Singh an hour after disembarking in Bombay that first time; like many Sikhs he was a tall man for an Indian, with the square shoulders and martial erectness of his people; his mobile, intelligent face was framed between a black turban and a black, carefully tended beard which I later learned he kept in a net when he slept.

Within a week he and Mulk Raj Anand had between them introduced us to all the local writers, artists and film makers of note. A couple of weeks later, in Delhi, Patwant performed the same service all over again with almost Mogul lavishness, giving enormous parties to which everyone came because nobody wanted to be left out. There we met not only great Indian writers like R.K. Narayan, the superb novelist from Mysore, but also great foreign writers, like the poet Octavio Paz, who was then Mexico's ambassador in Delhi.

Patwant's social adeptness and his love of pleasure made one think of him in those days – days that extended over the first decade and a half of our friendship – as the intelligent playboy, capable of writing a good book on Indian politics (he has since written three) and picking a good tailor on Savile Row, of editing an elegant magazine for sophisticates and wearing his highly starched turban in just as elegant combination with his Gucci shoes, all the while skittering as lightly as a skater over the tragic aspects of Asian existence.

About four years ago, all this changed dramatically, as it does so often with Indian men who approach the darker verges of middle age, and all at once become aware of the power of *karma* and the relation between present and future lives. Patwant suffered a heart attack. Recovering from it, he found himself considering what would have happened had he been a peasant farmer from one of the poverty-stricken villages near his country house at Ghamroj in Haryana, eighty kilometres or so from Delhi. Almost certainly he would have died, because there was no hospital near enough to save him. The thought nagged, as thoughts do in sleepless hospital nights, and when he had recovered, Patwant went out to look at the areas around his leisure farm with a new, uneasy eye. He found the villages poorer than he had thought, the land arid or desalinated from bad irrigation; eye diseases caused largely by vitamin deficiency were so prevalent that any child who

6

survived infancy had a ten-to-one chance of eventually contracting cataract or glaucoma; survival beyond infancy was itself reduced as a possibility by the high rate of gastroenteritis, and tuberculosis was on the upswing among cattle and hence among human beings; the women were still in semi purdah, living withdrawn and repressed lives inaccessible to family planning instruction, for though these people were Jats of Hindu faith, the area had for many centuries been under Muslim domination.

Returning from one of these pilgrimages into the foreign land that was his own country, Patwant had an experience that resembles any number of incidents from the legends of the Buddha's life. From his station wagon, Patwant saw a group of peasants by the roadside, obviously in distress. In their midst a young woman lay in agonized labour; she would die, it was evident, if she did not get help quickly. Patwant told the peasants to lift her into his car and had his driver go straight to the military hospital in Delhi; the woman's life and her child's were saved. The incident seemed like a sign. Patwant decided immediately to create a small hospital so that such a situation might never more arise among the peasants of Ghamroj. Looking vaguely into the future, he hoped others might be inspired by the example he proposed to set.

He got to work immediately, calling in the debts of years of lavish hospitality. He badgered the state government of Haryana into giving him a piece of land that he specified must be barren. He persuaded architect friends to design him an open campus of small pavilions that he could build cheaply out of local materials. He talked manufacturers into giving him beds and sheets and cement, almost the most sought-after commodity in modern Indian because not enough is produced to meet the demands of building, and what is available tends to be hoarded by profiteering merchants. He recruited retired army doctors to run his hospital and charmed Delhi specialists into offering services at nominal fees. He persuaded a couple of English nurses travelling in India to stay on and help set up the hospital and its extension services. And he turned to the vast international circle of friendships he had built up during his years of globe-trotting, and instituted annual pilgrimages to collect funds in Britain, in the United States, and especially in Canada, with its lumber-rich Vancouver Sikhs.

At this point, Inge and I became involved. As old friends who remembered what a cynical eye he had cast on our own efforts to resettle the Tibetan refugees, we were astonished at his transformation. But,

7

glad at long last that we were seeing as one, we got together a few other Old India Hands, some doctors, some other friends, and founded Canada India Village Aid. Tony Phillips, a professor of psychology at UBC, became our chairman, I became secretary, Inge contributed her experience in fund-raising, gathered when we worked for Tibetan refugees. When we started in 1981 we regarded Patwant Singh's hospital as a good venture in itself, and we hoped it might be replicable elsewhere in India, but our essential philosophy was worked out on the basis of Gandhi's idea of village regeneration being the real foundation for the revival of India, an idea long neglected by Indian politicians and sadly underplayed in Richard Attenborough's Establishment film, *Gandhi*. We hoped to extend our help beyond Patwant Singh's experiment, and in the four years since then we have done so; now there are village health projects we are helping in parts of India as distant from each other as Rajasthan in the northwest, Bihar in the northeast and Andhra Pradesh in the southeast. But that was still in the future when we decided to go to India in 1982.

Among the people attracted to our group was Toni Onley. Watching us working at banquets and book sales and garage sales to draw in money at a time when all charities were complaining of declining donations, Toni remarked: "It seems to me you're piddling away your energies to raise a few dollars. George, why don't you and I go to India together? I'll paint, you can write, we'll make a book together, and sell the paintings into the bargain."

I agreed, and this book you have in your hands began to take shape. I got out maps and reference books; we planned a trip with destinations we felt would show the great contrasts of India, that continent which masquerades as a country. Starting from Delhi, we would go into Rajasthan, to the cities far in the northwestern desert, and then south through Udaipur and Fatehpur Sikri to find the historic heart of India, the land of palaces and mosques and castled Rajput hills. Tony Phillips and Margo Palmer decided to join us on this part of our journey. Then we would fly far south to Kerala, with its lagoons and spice gardens, and stand at the tip of India, Cape Comorin, and afterwards cross the central plateau of the Deccan to the great temple complexes of Orissa. Continuing north through Calcutta, we would climb to Darjeeling with its Himalayan vistas and mountain way of life, and thence we would return to Delhi and so, via Burma, home. But first of all, we would visit Kabliji, which had given us the reason for our journey.

3. Fire in the Dust

Ghamroj, where the Kabliji Hospital had been built, lay on a secondary road out of Delhi on our way into Rajasthan. It was the kind of hopeless countryside that Inge and I already knew from having wandered around there in 1961 with Gandhian volunteers. The dusty soil, exhausted by three millennia of cultivation since the Aryans moved down from the mountains into the Jumna plain, now grew crops of stunted maize and of sugar cane four feet high. The peasants' adobe houses were so near to literal mud huts that we would often be aware of a village only when we were about to enter it, so closely did these settlements blend into the brown land. When we finally reached the hospital, in its patch of scrubby, salty ground, it had the same low-squatting look, the walls of its hexagonal buildings clad in fieldstone outside and whitewash within and roofed with lichened tiles from old British bungalows. Sitting on the beds in the wards, huddled under their grey-white cloaks, the sick peasants were able to look out at eye level on fields like their own, where teams of oxen limped to and fro, dragging wooden ploughs much like those used by Roman farmers two thousand years before.

The hospital's blending into the countryside was more than visual, for Patwant and his aides were setting out to change the way of life that sent these peasants crowding into the creeper-shaded pergola which served as an outpatients' waiting area. They had gone out into the twenty-six villages (population 200,000) served by the tiny hospital with its twenty-bed eye ward and its twenty-bed general ward (and a six-bed obstetrical ward to come later from Canada India Village Aid). They had met with the village *panchayats* (the traditional councils of five men dating from the reign of Ashoka in the third century B.C. and perhaps even earlier), and had advised and helped them with such basic tasks of municipal hygiene as paving the muddy tracks that served as roads, covering the open, fly-encrusted drains, lining the ancient wells that had become disease-infested deathtraps, and building latrines in the schoolyards. They would also be starting classes for retarded children. All this, the entirely male *panchayats* pointed out, needed cash; they had no cash to spare. But they did, as Patwant pointed out, have women living behind house doors with time on their hands, and when he brought in looms and yarn and arranged to sell the rugs that might be woven, the women emerged from the isolation of purdah to weave for clear wells and cleanliness so that their children should no longer die young of gastroenteritis. In the process, these village women would weave their own liberation.

By the time of our 1982–83 visit, we found that in some villages the sewers were already covered, the lanes paved, and clean, safe water was being drawn up from ancient wells that had been cleared out and rejuvenated. And, in big old houses deserted by absentee landlords, we heard the drywood clank of handmade looms, and the light chatter of knitting machines. We halted in doorways decorated with ancient patterns of moulded plaster, and lifted our joined hands in the *namaskar* gesture of greeting, as we waited for the women in their bright red and yellow best saris to garland us with sacred marigolds and dab our brows with auspicious red powder, and offer us sweet chunks of the fudge-like milk candy called *burfi*. Then they would invite us in to see the work that has changed the lives of women in such villages forever.

In the open courtyards hung with the bright-patterned dhurries – oblong rugs two yards by one – that were woven there, we found women of all ages at work: teenage girls at the knitting machines, matrons at the looms, old women preparing the yarn for dyeing and weaving. Within a few months of the looms appearing, the last vestiges of purdah had vanished in a quiet village revolution, and the women had begun to assume a more active role in village life. Another significant change had been a steady rise in the age of marriage, from fourteen or fifteen to nineteen or twenty, as young girls realized they now had earning powers. This meant an immediate dramatic reduction in the local birth rate. Even the status of widows, the traditional pariahs of Indian villages, has improved since the hospital began to employ them as aides and give them a rank in the community.

The effort throughout has been to foster change within the community itself, which is why, instead of sending paramedics into the villages from outside, the Kabliji Hospital has chosen to train the *dais*, or local traditional midwives, in simple hygiene and medicine so that new influences can enter village life through customary channels. In such ways this voluntary institution, devised by a man of imagination and resourcefulness, has done more to raise the quality of village life in this neglected corner of a neglected region than government agencies have done during all the thirty-five years since India became independent.

As we drove out of the compound at Kabliji, a cart drawn by white oxen with blue-painted horns was coming in: a man lay in it, wrapped almost to the eyes in a dirt-grey cotton cloth, so that we could not tell his age, but the woman who squatted beside him on the jolting floor of the cart held the fold of her faded green sari over her face, leaving only her eyes visible; she was one of the old school, unchanged as yet by the new spirit of Kabliji. Yet whatever was wrong with the man – and the boy driving the cart shrugged when our driver asked him – he had a hope that would not have existed four years earlier, before Kabliji was built, when the only recourse for a sick old peasant in one of these villages was a distant hospital he could not hope to reach.

The old people represented the past: India as it had been and so often still is. Kabliji looked into the problematical future: India as it might be if men of vision somehow gain control over its destinies. In between, along the roads and airways we would follow in the next weeks, was the changing India of the present with all its political confusions and its obstinate social anachronisms, its many faces and its many walls.

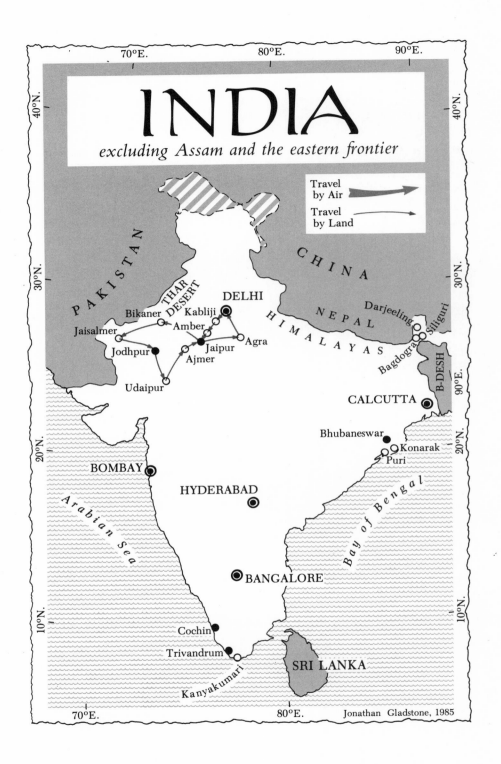

INDIA

excluding Assam and the eastern frontier

Travel by Air

Travel by Land

PAKISTAN

CHINA

THAR DESERT

DELHI

NEPAL

HIMALAYAS

Darjeeling

Siliguri

Bagdogra

B-DESH

Bikaner Kabliji

Jaisalmer Amber

Agra

Jodhpur Jaipur

Ajmer

Udaipur

CALCUTTA

Bhubaneswar

Konarak

Puri

BOMBAY

HYDERABAD

Arabian Sea

Bay of Bengal

BANGALORE

Cochin

Trivandrum

SRI LANKA

Kanyakumari

Jonathan Gladstone, 1985

II

RAJASTHAN

4. The Abode of Kings

More than most Indian regions, Rajasthan has resisted the forces of political and social homogenization that in recent years have been so greatly transforming India. The state, which less than forty years ago was a mosaic of independent principalities, is even now thinly populated by Indian standards (25 million people in more than 340 thousand square kilometres), and its people are largely scattered over deserts and among tortuous hill ranges and small mountains that in the Aravallis rise to almost six thousand feet above sea level. Throughout history, Rajasthan has remained off the main routes of trade and conquest. The invading Greeks of ancient times and the Muslims of the Middle Ages bypassed it to the north. The battles by which the British sealed their rule over India were fought in other parts of the subcontinent. Throughout the turbulent centuries of Indian history, Rajasthan remained a remoteness where those who were irreconcilable with the prevailing authority could take refuge, and it is out of such irreconcilables that the ruling race of the Rajputs seems to have evolved.

Rajasthan means "the abode of kings," and the Rajputs all claim descent from the Aryan chieftains who came out of central Asia more than three millennia ago to destroy the ancient civilizations of the Indus valley and to establish in their place a rule of warrior horsemen, the Kshatriya caste celebrated in legend as the heroes of those great epics, the *Ramayana* and above all the *Mahabharata*. But the original Kshatriya caste seems to have virtually destroyed itself during the civil wars that are condensed in legend into the great slaughter on the battlefield of Kurukshetra which is the climax of the *Mahabharata*, in rather the same way as the medieval nobility of England destroyed itself in the recurrent battles of the Wars of the Roses.

The historic Rajputs seem to be the descendants of a number of warrior peoples who retreated into the hills and deserts west of the Jumna and south of Punjab during the turbulent era between the appearance of Alexander the Great on the Indus in 326 B.C. and the death of Christ, when invader after invader pushed down over the Hindu Kush, established a temporary kingdom and then was swept away by his invading successors: the Bactrian Greeks, the Sakas, the Parthians, the Kushanas, the terrible White Huns. In their deserts and mountains, the remnants of all these peoples mingled and coalesced and hived off into the groups that became the Rajput clans, some claiming legendary descent from the sun deity and others from the moon deity. Fragmentary remnants of the ancient Kshatriya caste may indeed have survived, and perhaps the clans grouped around them, so it is possible that the Rajput princes themselves were the descendants of the warriors who fought, so legend says, with Krishna and Arjuna at Kurukshetra so long ago.

As identifiable groups, the Rajputs enter history only in the early Middle Ages, ruling kingdoms in the north of India and, under leaders who became figures of legend like Prithviraja, offering resistance to the waves of Muslim conquerors who from the eleventh century onwards poured into India over the traditional invasion route through Afghanistan. Prithviraja and his cause were destroyed by the weakness that had been the nemesis of the heroes of the *Mahabharata*: disunity. Even under the threat of Muslim invasion, he and his fellow Rajput kings remained at war with each other, and though he won one great victory over the invaders at Tarain in the last decade of the twelfth century, Prithviraja was soon afterwards defeated and killed on the same battlefield because the other princes would not support him. Clan loyalties were both the strength and the weakness of the Rajputs, inducing fierce resistance when local strongholds were threatened, but creating rivalries between the princes which were fatal to the role legend has given the Rajputs as defenders of the Hindu way of life against infidel invaders.

After the battles of the twelfth century, the Rajput kingdoms of the Jumna and Ganges valleys were eliminated, and the only rivals the Islamic rulers of Delhi had to fear were other Muslims coming by the same route to overthrow them and found other dynasties. But the Rajputs as a people did not vanish. They retreated to the narrow defensible valleys of the Himalayan foothills, around Kulu and Kangra, and to the mountains of Rajasthan and the Thar desert to the northwest of them, where thirst was a great ally against invading armies. There they built their forts, established their small realms, and kept their Hindu culture alive in the face of the Muslim threat by a variety of means, ranging from the stubborn military resistance of the Maharanas of Mewar (later Udaipur), the senior princes of the solar line, to the compromises by which the rulers of Amber and Bikaner not only survived and protected their traditions, but also prospered as mercenary generals of the Great Mogul. The tradition continued under the British, many of whose best Indian regiments were recruited among the Kshatriya or hereditary warrior caste of the Rajput native states.

*   *   *

We drove out from Ghamroj toward Jaipur, which is now the capital of Rajasthan, across the broad monotonous plain of the Jumna valley, the region where the Rajputs had fought their disastrous medieval battles before retreating into the jagged and barren hinterland.

We travelled in two cars which had been rented for us by the driver of one of our friends in Delhi. They belonged to a stocky Sikh, bearded and turbaned, named Surgit Singh, who had served in the army and knew some English. The cars were Ambassadors, a utilitarian but never very comfortable Indian make. Surgit claimed they were new; we very soon realized they were not. Surgit himself drove one of the cars and a tall, shy, silent man, a shaven Sikh called Ranjit, drove the other; he spoke no English, and we communicated with the odd fragments of Hindi that Inge and I had picked up on our travels. We solved the problem of three couples in two cars by alternating every day, so that in each car there would always be one couple and one odd person, couples riding together two days out of three.

In December the plain was almost colourless, the dun brown of a soil worked over by generations of cultivators, splashed here and there by the vivid squares of flowering mustard fields. The trees were also flowerless, sleeping their winter sleep; only the bougainvilleas played at summer with their papery false blossoms of coloured leaves that ranged the spectrum from orange through to purple.

The landscape was still mainly that of traditional India: mud-walled villages, little granaries of cane with conical roofs, peasants ploughing with oxen. But the road seemed to proclaim another culture, as top-heavy trucks painted gaudily with emblems of the Hindu gods pushed their great hulks through the diesel-permeated air to the sound of horns that were never silent. The traffic had overwhelmed the quiet roadside villages that we remembered on this road from twenty years before. On the edge of each settlement an agglomeration of makeshift shacks had grown up: traders' booths of worn and stained planks that looked like packing cases on stilts and were not much bigger; rough cane-roofed shelters posing as restaurants and surrounded by dozens of rope beds where the truck drivers sat cross-legged, drinking tea and eating curry, or lay napping beside the noisy road; little repair shops surrounded by the debris of cannibalized cars and trucks, for India still has a make-use-and-mend economy.

Gently, each side of the clamorous river of the road, the country changed. There was no abrupt entry into Rajasthan; more than anything else, we saw a steady drying of the land. Camel began to replace oxen, drawing carved and painted carts, dragging Roman-style ploughs, craning long necks to nibble twigs from the neem trees that sometimes turned the road into a shady avenue. Dormant rivers slashed the landscape with their arid trenches of shingle and sand. At some unnamed spot a small fort rose from a knoll overlooking the highway, its structure as solid and expert-looking as any castle of the Rhine or Danube. We were at last in the abode of kings and warriors, of those who built their castles not only for utility, but also because they loved the hard and solid grandeur of military architecture. Even the first Mogul emperor, Babur, looking at the Rajput forts with the expert eye of a soldier, referred to them as "wonderful buildings," and the princes competed in boasting of the impregnability of their forts. The greatest was the enormous stronghold of Chittorgarh in the state of Udaipur, whose rulers boasted that "Only Chittorgarh is a real fort, for it cannot be captured; the rest are just castles." But in the sixteenth century Chittorgarh too was captured by the forces of the Mogul emperor Akbar, though its defenders fought to the death.

Now the land began to rise into ridges of low hills, as if it had been whipped into waves by some cosmic tempest. They were densely furred by a dwarf forest of small-leaved scrub that reminded me of the obsessive imaginary forests painted by Ivan Eyre. Probing their defiles, the road reached the real frontier of Rajput country at the little town of Amber, where ruined walls clambered hundreds of feet up the steep infringing slopes. Beyond the conical towers of Amber's temples, a great yellow stone palace clung on a hillside, and above it, topping the high ridge, a stark dark fortress looked back toward the plain we had just crossed.

We went on through Amber and up the hill-ringed valley to Jaipur; in the city's outskirts we found big high-ceilinged rooms in the Rambagh Palace, one of the several lavish residences from which the Maharajahs of Jaipur once ruled their state. An early twentieth-century rendering of traditional Rajput architecture – domes and airy pavilions, draughty corridors and park-like formal gardens – it had become an

17

international hotel of the kind one now finds in large Indian cities. Such a hotel is distinct from its kind elsewhere only by virtue of its exotic setting, the traditional liveries of its servants, and a certain nonchalance that results from the fact that the Rajputs are not servile by nature; their attitude may vary in its manifestation from an easy courtesy to an irritating casualness in meeting one's requests. At the Rambagh Palace the local celebrant, perhaps rightly, always seemed to have precedence over the alien visitor. It took me half an hour to get tea on the terrace when a group of Rajput women, as brilliant as parrots in their vivid skirts and shawls, occupied the waiter with endless requests. And the night of a wedding party, it was impossible to get a drink for two hours and we were forced to fall back on our private store of whisky as we stood out on the lawns, in the light of blazing woodfires, and watched the queues of men in polyester suits going up to the platform, where the bride sat in her gold and scarlet mantle and the groom in his cloth-of-gold turban with its diamond aigrette and received discreet envelopes of money from the wedding guests. Patience and a due sense of the irrelevance of time are useful attitudes for the traveller in Rajasthan, as they are in most of India.

But this book is not a guide to hotels and their virtues or defects. As travellers out to observe and record, we found the Rambagh Palace most interesting as an example of the decadence that overwhelmed Rajput life during the long age of the Pax Britannica. Deprived of their favourite sport of warring with each other, the princes of Rajasthan had now to be content with ruling their states – in theory, absolutely, but in fact, under the watchful eyes of the British Residents – and with spending conspicuously on palaces and pastimes, among which, at Jaipur, polo was dominant. The last reigning Maharajah, a charming, sporty man I met in the 1960s, actually died of heart failure on the polo field; today his son, known generally in India as "Bubbles," carries on the polo-playing tradition.

When their states were incorporated in the new republican India, their powers and privileges vanished, their wealth shrank, and Rajasthan's princes joined the world's great company of needy aristocrats. In the years after their collective fall from office, the palaces they could not afford to maintain provided ready-built structures for the early stages of India's developing hotel industry. Thus, in almost every city of Rajasthan we would enjoy the decaying splendour and antiquated facilities of such princely follies.

In Jaipur, Toni and I took our first passes at the prose and painting for this book. Downed the day after our arrival by troubled intestines, Toni staggered out in the sun's setting brilliance – astonishing me, not for the last time, by the toughness of his dedication to painting – to sketch in the gardens of the Rambagh Palace an atmospheric trans-mutation of the building's walls and domes and pinnacles, set in the lush greenery of a well-tended Indian garden. At about the same time, I started to note the recollections of our days in India in one of those fat, square books of ruled paper one can still buy in the bazaar for a couple of rupees. These were mere beginnings – the tunings of the instruments – and it was in Amber next day that our work really began, which was appropriate, for there we were touching the roots of tradition and history among the Rajputs.

5. The Apes of Amber

The name of Amber has nothing to do with the fossilized resin that shares it; conjecture not very convincingly suggests it was derived from Ambikeshwar, a name of the great god Siva. But at least one analogy can be wrung out of the similarity of names, since in much the same way as the gum called amber preserved insects within its translucent globules, the place called Amber encapsulates much of the common history of the Rajputs. Once it was the stronghold of a tribal people, the Minas, who lived there long before the Aryan invaders reached India. In the eleventh century, under pressure of Muslim intrusion, the Kachhawa clan of Rajputs came westward out of central India. Led by Dhola Rai, who claimed descent from the Lord Rama, they found in the hills around Amber a good place to fortify and defend. They built the great walls up the hillsides and established a kind of symbiotic relationship with the Minas, who became their aides and allies. Dhola Rai is a figure of legend as well as history, as most of the old Rajput kings became, and his love for his beautiful queen, Marooni, is the subject of ballads remembered to this day by the Rajputs who, like most warrior peoples, set great store by romantic and impetuous love.

Compared with some of the Rajput clans, like the Sisodias of Mewar and the Rathors of Jodhpur, the Kachhawas of Amber were at first a minor lineage, playing a small role in the turbulent history of north-western India until the arrival of the Moguls and the reign of Akbar, who sought to turn the Rajputs from troublesome enemies into useful allies. The Sisodias of Mewar resisted both his overtures and his armies, with the result that their great fortress of Chitor in southern Rajasthan was several times besieged and sacked and the Maharana himself became a fugitive among the Bhil tribesmen of the Aravalli hills. But other Rajput princes, notably the rulers of Bikaner and Amber, accepted the friendship extended by Akbar, the Great Mogul, who reigned from 1556 to 1605. Man Singh not only offered his warriors as mercenaries, he became one of Akbar's leading generals himself, and even gave his daughter to the Mogul, who shrewdly sealed with marriage all his alliances with the Hindu princes.

From this accommodation with Akbar – continued by his successors under the later Moguls – Man Singh gained wealth and power. Moreover, in the courts of Fatehpur Sikri and Agra, he saw the elegance of living and setting that the Muslim rulers had brought with them from Persia. Like other Rajput princes, he decided to supplement the dour starkness of warriors' fortresses on desert rocks with the grace of palaces built for the refined leisure that the stability of Akbar's reign allowed. In 1592 he began to build the palace on the hill above the old town of Amber; it was not finished until nearly 150 years later, in the early reign of his descendant, Sawai Jai Singh, the founder of Jaipur.

Coming from Jaipur back to Amber, we saw the great golden structure of the palace reflected in the lake below, and here, under the tamarind trees on its shore, Toni settled down to paint. He carried a wooden case of his own design that served in combination as a paintbox, a container for paper and finished paintings, a palette and a knee-held easel; a jar of clear water was all he needed to set up in the desert or the mountains or anywhere else. While he and Yukiko stayed beside the lake, the rest of us went up the zigzag hillside road to the palace. When Inge and I first reached Amber in 1961, the only way up that road was on foot or lurching on elephant back. Now the road was open to cars, but not many used it, and the elephants, swaying their cargoes of visitors uphill and downhill, were still there, wearing their elaborate silver brow ornaments, their faces and trunks painted in delicately complex patterns of flowers and stars, and, at nature's call, their cannonball turds falling steaming from under their tufty tails. "Elephant ride," noted the locally published guidebook I had bought in the Jaipur bazaar, "is a Royal experience and a good enjoyment."

When we reached the great square before the palace and climbed the broad, familiar stairs from terrace to terrace, passing under the massive gateways and wandering under the latticed galleries of the great halls, I found myself making comparisons with our previous visit in terms of decaying splendour. The miniatures on the walls were more faded, the mirror work a shade more blurred than I remembered it; down by the sinister old gate where, long ago, the princesses went out to be burned on their husbands' pyres, the pathetic marks of their hennaed hands, still visible when we first came to Amber, had been painted out by someone who did not want the world to be reminded of one of the more savage aspects of the Rajput past.

I was carrying my old book, *Faces of India*, with me, and in a quiet little room of the *zenana*, I opened it at the page where, so many years before, I had recorded my first impressions of Amber.

> As a feature of the landscape, a great pile of yellow stone crowning its hilltop and already feeling the bite of time, the Amber palace is impressive. But inside the gates, every arch seemed heavy and earthbound in comparison with the soaring lightness that the Mogul architects achieved. The charms of Amber were in detail and on the surface, the charms of painting and well-laid mosaic softened by age. By the time Man Singh began to build his palace, Indian artists had become either decorators, and in that role conservative and imitative, or, where the strain of originality persisted, miniaturists. The best of Amber was the work of its decorators and miniaturists; the worst was the work of its architects.

I would not change that judgment. But I would add that in spite of the heaviness of those early arches and the imitativeness of the decorations – hardly yet differentiated from Mogul work – the palace of Amber is still remarkably evocative of a past period and its life, and largely because, unlike so many princely palaces in Rajasthan, it is a monument without being a museum. There is nothing left there of the strange miscellaneous clutter that the native princes hoarded like pack-rats before their rule came to an end in 1947. But the space that contained their lives remains and calls on the mind for echoes to fill it.

Amber, and all the splendour of the Rajput past, were new to Tony and Margo, and they were anxious to wander through the buildings and photograph them. Inge was content to sit in the sun and watch the visitors, and I wanted to wander on my own and regather my thoughts on India.

I walked through the empty halls and mirrored chambers, and my imagination began to roam and look out through the stone lattices and feel the cool air blowing in through the elegant perforated marble screens and build its free images of the past. One windowed turret looked down to the lake and the elegant little water palace beside it, with a garden whose low stone walls made star-shaped beds now choked with grass and moss instead of being filled with the pinks and roses whose flowers the Rajputs loved. I was reminded of a marvellous painted Rajput hanging we bought in Calcutta twenty years ago and still have on the wall of our house, which depicts a series of five formidable warriors, each holding a pink in his hand and sniffing it.

Out across the lake I saw Toni painting with absorption in a circle of curious cows, and I wondered into what grand and simple forms of architecture merging with virgin rock he would be transforming this grandiose building whose multitude of internal details I had been attempting to assimilate. From another turret I looked down on the narrow, muddy lanes of Amber and the spires of its temples and the minarets of the mosque Akbar had built there in his effort to bring all religions into that simple unity of which he believed each was an aspect. The walls ran in every direction up the hills. The forts and watchtowers glowered, even in the noon sunlight. For all his alliance with Akbar, Man Singh was obviously not a man to take chances. Like all the Rajput princes, he saw his security and independence in terms of walls – the higher and thicker the better.

The princes and the princesses and the courtiers had long gone, and the palace's most noticeable inhabitants were now a tribe of large, grey langur monkeys, playing over the roofs and from the walls critically watching the visitors, many of whom were the simple village people of India who recently have begun to take an interest in their past and visit monuments and museums. Some of the women visited the little silver-doored temple to the goddess Kali that stands in a corner of the main courtyard. Like other malign deities, Kali has power over childbirth and the women queued up to ring the bell before the sanctuary and to put money in the silver chest that stood beside it. A priest, his brow painted with the trident symbol of Siva the "benevolent", handed to each a garland of marigolds and a *prasad* – a blessed gift – consisting of a little cardboard box tied with ribbon and containing sacred sweetmeats. The monkeys – themselves sacred – lurked outside the temple, cadging food from the people who came out and watching for anything they could snatch. One young woman, large-eyed and innocent, they marked as their prey; three of them attacked her at once, seizing in their strong hands her wreath, her holy sweetmeats and her purse. The purse was torn open and thrown with its pathetic contents far over the pavement; the floral wreath and the sweets were immediately eaten. The woman wept; she had paid ten rupees to the priest for her holy gift, a great deal for a poor villager. And the fact that a sacred monkey should steal the gifts of the priest must have appeared a dreadful omen; the child she hoped for would not be born. But nobody attempted to chastise or chase away the monkeys, for they, after all, were the people of the monkey king Hanuman who, in the far and legendary past, led his legions of apes to the assistance of Rama, the forefather of the Rajputs. Legend and history, imagined origins and real past, mingle inextricably in the Indian consciousness, and the present is shaped as much by what could not have taken place as by what actually happened.

6. The Astronomer Prince

All through the seventeenth century, the high age of the Moguls, the Kachhawa princes remained in Amber, extending their palace and accumulating wealth from their military services. But they distrusted the power those capricious emperors wielded from their Red Forts – first in Agra and then in Delhi – enough to stay within the knot of their protective hills. Only in the eighteenth century, as the power of the Moguls began to decline, did Sawai Jai Singh, perhaps the greatest and certainly the most imaginative of the rulers of Amber, decide to move into the open, down to the broad valley south of his old fortress town.

Sawai Jai Singh had been close to the heart of Mogul affairs, under a succession of emperors from the cruelly pious Aurangzebe at the outset of the eighteenth century, whose Islamic fanaticism began to alienate his Hindu allies and created the first rifts in the empire Akbar had so sensibly governed, down to Muhammed Shah, under whose rule the Muslim provincial governors became virtually independent, the Hindu Marathas emerged as a powerful military presence from the dry hills of the Deccan, and Nadir Shah, the usurper of the Persian throne, marched in 1737 into Delhi and sat on a high place to watch thirty thousand of its people massacred before he departed, carrying the treasures of the Red Fort, including Shah Jehan's splendid Peacock Throne.

Sawai Jai Singh was a capable general and a fine scholar, but also a clever courtier and reputed to be a ruthless intriguer. Certainly he perceived the opportunity that the weakening of Mogul rule gave local princes to aggrandize themselves without fear of retribution, so long as they did so with an eye to the rising menace of the Marathas, who, like the Sikhs to the north in the Punjab, were trying to spread a Hindu power – even if a somewhat heretical one on the part of the Sikhs – over large parts of India as Muslim power decayed. As a Rajput, Sawai Jai Singh was unwilling to bow to either of these groups of militarized peasants whom the disorder of India had allowed to assume the role of warriors, and in 1727, when he started to build Jaipur in the plain, he also built watchtowers and forts in the hills around it, including the massive Tiger Fort which he began to construct in 1734, only seven years after starting on his city, so rapid was the disintegration of India at this time and so urgent the need for good walls against the future.

The incorporation of the state of Jaipur into free India brought an end to the architectural extravagances of its rulers, but there were more than two good building centuries from Sawai Jai Singh's day down to 1947. On the road south from Amber, we were constantly reminded – by strong walls on distant hilltops or by graceful structures in the valley – of the vast amounts of money and labour the princes had used, first to protect their realms and then, during the Pax Britannica, to enhance the splendour of their hollow authority.

There was Tiger Fort itself, its dark and massive walls glowering from an arid hilltop over the city it was built to defend, and on the next hill the castle-like structure of the Sun Temple, tutelary shrine of the Kachhawa rulers, its white spire glistening against the blue sky and its high yellow enclosing wall painted with a great white swastika, the symbol of the sun cult of the Rajputs.

In the flat land of the valley, princely buildings, in a later and lighter Rajput style than that of Amber, were scattered among the winter-brown ploughed fields: little temples, pavilions, even palaces. At Gaitor, in walled gardens among mango trees on which the first modest but splendidly scented blossoms were just beginning to open, stood the cenotaphs of the Kachhawa princes. These were not tombs. The bodies of the princes had been burnt – and often their living princesses with them – and their ashes scattered in the Ganges, but something must remain to commemorate departed splendour, and so the Rajputs had traditionally built these very elegant memorial pavilions. Sawai Jai Singh himself was remembered in a structure of white marble: delicately carved fences enclosing a rococo chhatri, a dome suspended on air and four slender pillars.

Jal Mahal Palace, Jaipur

Jalmahal Palace, Jaipur, India. December 1994

Amber Fort over Masta Lake

Amber Fort over Masta Lake, India, December 17 1982

Garden, Junagarh Fort, Bikaner

Garden, Fort Junagarh, Bikaner, India December 13 1982

Junagarh Fort,' Bikaner

Junagarh Fort, Bikaner, India, Dec. 19, 1902

For relaxation in the hot months while he was engaged in the great task of constructing Jaipur, Sawai Jai Singh built just south of Gaitor a Jal Mahal or Water Palace. On our first visit in 1961, it had struck a romantic chord in my mind, and I wrote in *Faces of India* that "among the reedbeds beside a lake like a flat disc of turquoise rose a deserted structure as frail and romantic as a vanishing fairy castle of Tennysonian legend ..." Now, in 1982, I saw the Jal Mahal again, but the turquoise water in which it had once been reflected was no longer visible. The palace seemed to stand up – and looked solid rather than frail because it had no reflection – out of a vast field of coarse and dark green foliage. It was only when I saw the heads of water buffalo appearing among the leaves that I realized the lake I had seen then – in the middle of which Sawai Jai Singh had built his Jal Mahal – had been invaded and choked during the last twenty years by a fast-spreading plague of water hyacinth.

But the magic of art is strange and devious. We left Toni and Yukiko near the Jal Mahal, beside a shallow and still unchoked pond inhabited by white and stilt-legged spoonbills, while the rest of us went back into Jaipur, and Margo and Inge bargained for mirror-work skirts in the bazaar outside the City Palace. That evening, in the Rambagh Palace, Toni showed me the painting he had made. At this time he had not read *Faces of India*, but by some intuition he had recognized the origin and function and also the mana of the structure he was painting, and what appeared was indeed, as I had seen long ago, "a deserted structure as frail and romantic as a vanishing fairy castle of Tennysonian legend ..."

*   *   *

The eighteenth century in India was a strange springtime of relations between East and West, a time when the two cultures came together with an innocence that was not repeatable. The French and the English were there in force, fighting each other for markets and influence. But as freebooters, which they still were, they were considerably more acceptable than merciless adventurers like Nadir Shah, and no farther removed from the Hindu majority than the Moguls or the Muslim viceroys who set themselves up as independent monarchs in the Deccan, Bengal and Oudh. The Marathas and the Sikhs often employed European officers to train and command their armies and, in those years before the dreaded memsahibs arrived, the relations between Indians and Europeans were socially far easier than they later became; marriages between them took place at this time which in the years after the Mutiny neither side would have countenanced.

Such military and marital accommodations were accompanied by exchanges in cultural influence. English philologists established the scholarly study of Sanskrit and other classic Indian languages, and English archaeologists, by finding his decrees inscribed on rocks, drew the mighty Ashoka out of the mists of legend, so that to a great extent the West gave back its past to the East during these initial decades of contact. And cultured Indians in their turn appropriated what to them seemed the best of European teachings, sometimes, as in the case of the Bengali Ram Mohun Roy who started a Hindu reform movement called Brahmo Samaj, in philosophic terms, and sometimes, as in the case of Sawai Jai Singh, in terms of applied science.

In various ways, through the Jesuits who attended the court of Akbar, and the English envoys who visited his son Jehangir, the ideas of the European Renaissance found their way – somewhat attenuated – to India; among them were the concepts of urban layout that had inspired the design of cities built after the Middle Ages drew to an end. There is no record telling from what wandering French or Italian or English adventurer Sawai Jai Singh gained his inspiration, but it is known that when he set out to construct his new capital – Jaipur, the city of Jai, named for himself – he obtained plans of towns constructed in Europe during the seventeenth and early eighteenth centuries, and employed Indian scholars to collate them with the instructions of the ancient Hindu treatises on design known as the *Silpasastras*. Out of such researches emerged the plan of the city that still stands within its original crenellated walls of rosy sandstone.

On entering Jaipur the sense of space and grandeur is remarkable. Going in from the north through the Korawar gate and driving along the Sirdeori Bazaar, with the City Palace and the strange structure of the Palace of the Winds to the left and the merchants' houses with their busy ground floor shops and latticed upper storeys to the right, one is not following the narrow lanes of some traditional Asian warren of a town, like the bazaar quarters of Old Delhi or Agra, but an open avenue 110 feet broad, joining similar avenues in wide market squares and crossed by secondary roads, themselves more than fifty feet wide.

Unfortunately, time has not dealt kindly with Sawai Jai Singh's concepts of town planning, so far ahead of anything else in eighteenth-century India, yet so vulnerable, because of their very openness, to twentieth-century invasions. Jaipur had the misfortune to be named the capital of the new state of Rajasthan, perhaps because it was the nearest Rajput city to Delhi. The promotion changed it from the little princely city it had still been in 1961, when Inge and I toured it in pony-drawn and bone-jolting gharries, because cabs were so few, into a busy and crowded provincial capital with nearly a million inhabitants.

The broad avenues that Sawai Jai Singh had laid out to aerate his city and give its people a sense of liberating space were now so jammed with cars that pony-drawn vehicles proceeded there only with great risk. The air was faintly blue with diesel fumes. Beyond the walls a vast suburban agglomeration had grown up, the wide streets imitating those of the old city, but everything else hideously unplanned. The Rambagh Palace, meant as a semi-rural retreat for the princes, now conserves the only park in an area of unregulated building in whose noisy torrent of traffic the camels try to maintain an air of disdainful contempt as they drag their carts among rickety buses with people hanging from their sides like bats on moving trees and gaudy motor-cycle rickshaws weaving their way perilously among the overloaded trucks. Sometimes, in a quieter street, a string of polo ponies trots by, on exercise; sometimes, gigantic and formidable even among the modern traffic, a work elephant pads along, its small eyes flicking from side to side with a look of incipient paranoia. But camels, elephants and polo ponies are vestiges of an almost vanished past. More than any other of the princely towns of Rajasthan, Jaipur has surrendered to the levelling homogenization that today afflicts all the major cities of India.

The single refuge, the place that has changed hardly at all over the years, is the vast enclosure of the City Palace, whose great wall, the Sarbad, encloses about a seventh of the old city. Once it was the ruling centre of the state, a Rajput miniature Kremlin, housing all the administrative offices as well as the prince's courtly entourage. Now it survives as a decentralized museum, with the seven-storey tower of the Chandra Mahal reserved as a residence for the former maharajah. The day we went there, his standard flying on the roof showed that he was present, so that we could not climb up, as we had done in the past, to the room on the highest floor where the rulers would sit on cloth-of-gold seats to worship their favourite deity who was, needless to say, Laksmi, the goddess of wealth.

Since that time, too, the fascinating miscellany of relics that filled the buildings has been weeded out as curatorial hands have turned them into something resembling modern museums. One no longer walks through rooms filled with insipid Empire furniture, and corridors crammed with French bronze nudes and steel engravings of Victorian durbars. Perhaps this does show off to better advantage the luminously brilliant Rajput miniatures celebrating the amorous adventures of Krishna and other legendary figures which the princes commissioned and collected, and the splendid Persian and Sanskrit manuscripts Sawai Jai Singh and the other more scholarly princes accumulated. But a certain excess was natural to Indian princedom, and cultivated by the maharajahs during the British era, undoubtedly with the half-conscious thought of making up with unlimited and eccentric spending for their absence of independent power. To hide the evidence of that excess may be aesthetically justified, but it is also a kind of historical falsification. We now see the maharajahs represented by their better selves; their baser or sillier personae are carefully painted out.

And that is perhaps why in the City Palace one is still attracted by the more outlandish and grandiose exhibits, such as the vast brocade ceremonial gowns of the great Man Singh, founder of Kachhawa fortunes, and the jewelled sword weighing eleven pounds that he wielded in his battles, or the two capacious silver vessels, shaped like melons but each higher than a tall man, in which one of the nineteenth-century rulers, visiting England, transported the water he would drink during his sojourn there, since he believed foreign tap water would be polluting for a devout Hindu.

The buildings of the City Palace have their own share of strangeness. The ladies of Sawai Pratap Singh's *zenana* complained of being secluded from all sight of the outside world, so in 1799 he constructed what is surely the most extraordinary false front in the world – the Hawa Mahal, Palace of the Winds, a triangular structure fronting the main bazaar street of the old city like a great honeycomb of latticed balconies, narrowing to the summit at the fifth floor, with nothing behind them but the access stairs, so that what from the street seems to be a large rococo palace is no more than an airy façade blown through by the winds that give the structure its name.

More serious in intent if even stranger in appearance is the Jantar Mantar, the great observatory which Sawai Jai Singh built in 1728, the year he began the construction of Jaipur itself. Jai Singh was, among his many other accomplishments, a notable amateur astronomer. He corresponded with European astronomers and is said to have corrected the errors in some of their calculations. He had Euclid's *Elements* and

Napier's *Logarithms* translated into Sanskrit for the use of Indian scholars. And he was so enthusiastic about the pursuit of astronomy that he constructed not one, but five of his extraordinary observatories; the first, built in 1724, was in Delhi, the others in Benares, in Ujjain, and in Mathura, all of them centres of Brahmin or Islamic scholarship. They are the strangest looking of all Indian monuments because they bear little relation to any of the traditions of either Muslim or Hindu religious or domestic architecture. They are projections in gigantic masonry of scientific calculations about the nature of the heavens, and though they obviously make great use of Hindu mathematics (a noble and largely unrecognized tradition), they remind one less of modern European astronomical equipment than of the great stone instruments for observing the movements of the sun and planets that were constructed by the megalith builders in distant prehistoric times. For each instrument is in fact a massive structure, the biggest among them a sundial whose gnomon is a masonry triangle ninety-eight feet high, creating a shadow that moves thirteen feet an hour. There are great ramps and stone circles and marble bowls chased with signs and symbols, each with its specific purposes of measuring the position of stars, calculating eclipses, and so on. Today they are still used for astrological purposes by some of the Brahmins. But the impact of the Jantar Mantar on the stranger seeing it for the first time is powerfully aesthetic; the assembly of massive geometric shapes looks like nothing so much as a Chirico painting put into three dimensions. Only the black-faced monkeys leaping up the steps of the gnomon and the tall-crested hoopoes probing with their long beaks into the lawns around the glistening marble bowls seemed to relate its frozen abstractions to the world of the living. For a Rajput, even the abstractions of the heavenly science came to be expressed in majestic and strangely shaped walls.

7. Palaces of Moon and Flowers

The peacocks calling with their harsh clamour in the gardens of the Rambagh Palace woke me on the morning we left Jaipur for the cities of the desert. The Thar desert stretches over the whole northwestern section of Rajasthan, and the journey to Bikaner, our first destination, was a progression into barrenness and aridity. Surgit Singh, our driver, put his hands together and silently prayed for a moment before he started the car and drove out of the palace grounds into the heavy Jaipur traffic, which we did not leave behind until we were well beyond the city bounds. City traffic held no fears for Surgit; he would slide his car, never halting and constantly hooting, through the thick of it like a fish passing through water, without showing the least perturbation. But though he made loud Sikh boasts to have driven over the whole of north India, it was soon quite evident that he had never been beyond Jaipur, and to him the Thar desert was terra incognita, the land of marvels and monsters.

Because so much of it is barren land, Rajasthan has a pattern of population very different from the fertile areas of India like the great Jumna-Ganges plain, where the villages lie close together – often little more than shouting distance apart. Twenty miles beyond Jaipur, the phrase "crowded India" has already become an insupportable cliché. In pre-independence Rajputana, there was usually a single real city or town in each state, dominated by the princely citadel; given the wretchedness of the soil and the high living of the rulers, this was all the land could usually sustain. There were isolated fortresses, always solidly morticed on to the virgin rock, on some of the hills, particularly in the vague borderlands between different states, but even at the high-roads, the more pacific kinds of settlement were rare and modest – villages for the most part, and not many of them. In the whole three hundred kilometres between Jaipur and Bikaner, we passed through only two modest communities that might be called towns, Sikar and Ratangar, and the country was so little populated that where road repairs were going on, the workers who chipped the stones with little hammers and put them into place by hand – for road machines are hardly known in India – lived in improvised encampments of ragged canvas tents and shelters made out of reed mats. These were people well on the far side of the poverty wall, earning about a dollar a day for their labour.

Around Jaipur there was still enough scrubby vegetation to maintain a surprising number of singularly brilliant birds – parakeets and barbets and rollers – but very soon the only trees were a kind of tamarind whose gnarled and angular branches resembled those of olives. The camels browsed their twigs, and in the hamlets of mud houses, the dust patches that passed for fields were fenced by long piles of the thorny boughs. Whatever agriculture went on was rudimentary, conducted with primitive tools like the two-pronged wooden forks, made from divided branches, that the peasants used to stack their millet straw.

This was the real camel country; loads were carried on the animals' backs rather than in carts, and red-turbaned men rode on their backs at a fast trot. The camels' presence had its own subtle effect on the landscape, or on one's perception of it, for as the country became more arid and open, their tracks going far off the road toward the horizon, where sand and sky seemed to blend into a turquoise haze, gave a haunting sense of unbounded distance.

When it finally surrounded us without a tree in sight, the desert became a pale tan colour, suffused by the dull green, almost grey, of the broom and dwarf thorn bushes and milkweed, whose stems Surgit warned us against picking, since their sticky juice could blind us if we rubbed our eyes after contact with it. It was a hostile landscape, yet it supported life. Once, in the most desolate part, we encountered three boy shepherds, with a dozen black and white goats, a hundred sheep, and a pack donkey on which they carried their provender on the great circuits they made to find the green shoots to feed their flock. They followed the rain and the seasons for many miles, but always in circles that narrowed back to their village. They were wandering shepherds, not true nomads.

Bikaner is not one of those grandly spectacular Rajput places standing in lordly height above the barren land. We slid almost surreptitiously into the city between great army camps, with Russian cannon and tanks hidden under camouflage nets among the dunes; Bikaner is a mere 192 kilometres from the frontier that parts the Thar desert from the desert of Sind in Pakistan. The presence of the army is not unwelcome for, apart from business, Bikaner has its own military traditions. It was the headquarters of the celebrated Camel Corps which Maharajah Sir Ganga Singh led to assist the British in China during the Boxer rebellion and to Somaliland to fight the Mad Mullah and his dervishes. Nowhere under the Raj were there stronger defenders of the imperialism that protected them than the Rajput princes. Ganga Singh was regarded as so impeccably loyal that he was invited to take part in the Versailles peace conference in 1919 as one of the Indian representatives, and appears picturesquely in William Orpen's famous painting of the world statesmen assembled for that unpropitious event.

In Rajasthan one travels from princely home to princely home, and in Bikaner we stayed in the Lalgarh Palace, another creation of Sir Ganga Singh, a red sandstone building of spacious wings and courtyards in which the classic late Rajput style of the eighteenth century was faithfully followed by craftsmen who still worked in the tradition. Wherever one wandered, there were beautifully intricate stone lattices,

elegant turrets at the turnings of walls, gay little chhatris over the
gateways. Not that one could wander unimpeded; when Inge and I
went beyond a certain invisible mark on a dried-up lawn, a figure in
a ragged khaki greatcoat leapt up from a charpoy on which he had been
napping to wave an ancient firearm and point to a sign that read *Voie
Privée*. Beyond that notice, with its suggestion of nostalgia for lost days
of princely frivolity on the Côte d'Azur, the present maharajah lived,
theoretically untitled but holding his place in the hearts of good Rajputs,
those martial men with jutting moustaches and the names of lions who
regard the democratic rulers of modern India with a mixture of re-
sentment and contempt. Here, the maharajah would be called Bikaner
because in India one calls a reigning prince – or a prince who would
be reigning if native states still existed – by the name of his state. Indeed,
I once earned great disapproval when I talked to another Rajput about
the Maharajah of Surket, whom I knew quite well, and called him by
his actual name, Lalit Sen. The other Rajput gave me a withering look
and said: "I presume you mean Surket?" I think the fact that the princes
have lost their realms means that they are even more intent on the titles
to them.

   In the Rambagh Palace we had encountered a valiant attempt to
reconcile Hilton-style hotelmanship with the ambiance of the Arabian
Nights. In the chambers of the Lalgarh Palace there were no such
ambitions; instead, we endured the slow death of the Edwardian Raj.
Our rooms were scattered along dim and lofty corridors through which
bats flew twittering after nightfall. Immense old padlocks had to be
removed from their doors, before we could enter them. Within were
marble floors and great mahogany fireplaces, brass-steaded beds, rickety
walnut furniture, and pale Victorian watercolours of English woodlands
hanging on the damp-mottled wallpaper where gecko lizards clung and
talked in clicks. Inge and I complained because we had no wardrobe
in our room; and so the rustic boy who acted as bearer brought a second
stag-horn coat stand. But we had two bathrooms, equally useless, for
in one the antique tangle of pipes and taps, like a bizarre metal bird's
nest, had long ceased to work and rust had eaten in great wounds
through the enamel on the bath, while in the other the new washbasin
and toilet had been installed by some desert plumber so enamoured of
the drip of water that he had neglected to seal the joints and we padded
around in a perpetual shallow pool. The battles of eighteenth-century
India were commemorated in prints hung in the corridors with shabby
cloth curtains to protect them from the sun. The cul-de-sac where Toni

and Yukiko had their room was hung with dusty and barbaric mementos of the imperial past: the skins of gigantic tigers and leopards, the heads of formidable sambar and rhinoceros.

It all belonged to a far shabbier and less creative age than the more bloody times when Bikaner – whose rulers also became generals for the Moguls – flourished under Akbar and his successors. This became evident when we compared the apology for a museum in the Lalgarh Palace with the splendour – even diminished – of the vast old Junagarh Fort in the heart of the city. The later maharajahs showed themselves true sons of the camera age, for the Lalgarh museum was little more than a vast family album stuck on the stone pages of the walls in a whole palace wing. The princes, recent and past, stood among the carnage whose relics decorated Toni's corridor; they placed booted feet on the heads of splendid Bengal tigers, stood on the mounded backs of downed elephants, posed beside hills of slaughtered sandgrouse, usually with friends of the ruling race: Curzon or a lesser viceroy, or that perpetual jaded boy, Edward, Prince of Wales. Morally, of course, there is not much difference between basing one's prestige on the slaughter of many men and basing it on the slaughter of many animals; the unnecessary taking of lives is always repugnant. Nevertheless, these scenes of bloody vanity had a peculiar shoddiness that made one realize how far the Pax Britannica had diminished the fierce warrior rulers, even according to their own Kshatriya code.

By making Rai Singh of Bikaner and Man Singh of Amber generals in his army and accepting their daughters as imperial consorts (so that the emperor Jehangir was actually Rai Singh's grandson, Akbar created a kind of partnership in power, even if only a fleeting one, with the Rajputs. By depriving these former rulers of any sense of involvement in the fate of India beyond the bounds of their little states, and compensating with ceremonial concessions like the number of guns in their salutes, the British reduced them to titled flunkeys rather than true vassals. Ironically, though it broke its promises to them by tearing away the last of their privileges, the new Indian republic may have done its aristocrats a service in the end by giving them the status of equal citizens in a society where, paradoxically, the memory of their lost grandeur has given them the Orwellian dignity of being "more equal than others." In a world where rank and caste, like Johnny Walker, still go strong, to have been a maharajah counts. Yet I was so depressed by those photographs of aristocratic holocausts of beasts and birds that I could not bring myself to use the letter of introduction that would have taken me along the *Voie Privée* to the former ruler's part of the palace. That was perhaps unfortunate, for Bikaner has the reputation of being a capable and cultured man.

Until the fifteenth century, Bikaner was a mere oasis visited by nomadic herdsmen. Then, in 1488, Rao Bikaji, a younger son of the ruler of Jodhpur, conquered it to establish his own realm. Under his successors it became a halting point on one of the great caravan routes out of western Asia as well as a breeding centre whose fine camels were known and sought throughout northwestern India and the regions that now form the deserts of Pakistan. But, like Amber's, Bikaner's real prosperity came when Rai Singh accepted his role as a Mogul general and the perquisites that accompanied it, so that in the five years between 1588 and 1593 he was able to build the thousand-metre circuit of ramparts that walled his citadel of Junagarh in the heart of the city. Junagarh stands to this day, its red stone walls blackened by the lichen of centuries, a heart of resistance from which the horsemen and the camel riders of Maharajah Karn Singh rode out nearly three centuries ago to harry and defeat, among the dunes and the bitter wells of the desert, the army which the fanatical Mogul emperor Aurangzebe had sent in a futile attempt to change the relationship of the Hindu princes from the kind of partnership Akbar developed to a subordination aiming at the final victory of Islam in India.

Some of its original rocky grimness still clings to the fort. As we circled the walls and entered the Sun Gate, we saw there on the side wall the signs of the *sati* victims, made clear and permanent – as they had not been in Amber – by the stone having been cut away around the vermilion handmarks to throw them into cruel relief; no one in this desert city off the tourist circuit had tried to paint or plaster them over. Through that archway of death, one entered the ghost of a garden realm, for though Aurangzebe did not get near enough to breach the ramparts of Junagarh, the desert had mounted its own campaign, the lawns had gone back to dust, and in the orchards only the stubborn fig trees survived. Losing power and much of their wealth, the princes of Bikaner were unable to preserve every relic of their multichromatic past. But, like good Rajputs, they retreated into their citadels and held on stubbornly. The last maharajah to reign turned over Junagarh to the people of the city so that it should not fall into the still imperial hands of whoever rules in Delhi. A wisdom that developed between prince and people decreed that the gardens, which differed very little in style and form from those of other Rajput princes or of the Mogul overlords themselves, might be left to time and nature, while the ingenuities of human craft, which sometimes ascended into art, should be preserved.

For within the dark ramparts of Junagarh there were not only barracks and gardens, but also a whole succession of palaces, built and embellished by ruler after ruler, from sixteenth-century Rai Singh down to that nineteenth-century successor who ordered that murals be painted to celebrate the arrival of modern inventions in his desert remoteness. On one high wall in the heart of the fort, a naively painted locomotive drawing wagons filled with turbaned court dignitaries, top-hatted white men and bonnetted memsahibs, commemorates the arrival of the railway at Bikaner, an event that foretold the end of the camel caravans, and of the caravanserais, where merchants and their drivers stayed while they bargained with the Jain traders who lived under the protection of the Rajput rulers in a symbiosis that seems all the more strange when one remembers how far – as Kshatriyas – the Rajputs were from sharing the Jain doctrine of *ahimsa*, the non-doing of harm to all living beings.

The linked series of airily balconied, turreted, domed and poetically named structures within the formidable enclosure of Junagarh Fort – Moon Palace and Flower Palace and Glass Palace and so forth – celebrated the erotic element in the love-and-death complex of emotion and imagery which the Rajputs, reaching tangentially into the great curve of Indo-European culture, shared with hero-obsessed Homer and with the medieval European troubadours trapped in their dreams of knights without fear or reproach serving their ineffable *princesses lointaines*. Romantic longing, and the desire to capture and hold its evanescent transformations at the hands of artists who themselves are romantics, is a manifestation everywhere of aristocratic cultures that have gone beyond the stage where the warrior virtues of loyalty and courage are regarded as in themselves sufficient.

And everywhere in the palaces within the grim fort of desert Bikaner one senses this union of Eros and Thanatos: women who would go, for a sense of romantic attachment, to the funeral pyre; men who would don the saffron robe of renunciation and eat copiously of opium when pride and the needs of battle led them toward suicide; together in these elegant chambers, contriving and proclaiming on their coloured walls the life of erotic gaiety, of emotional intensity, that is embodied in the legends of the Lord Krishna and his many loves which so delighted the Rajput princes and their painters – the Lord Krishna whose jewelled swing in replica swayed in the topmost room of Junagarh Fort, the room to which the rulers and their consorts would retire for their lofty consummations

Other palaces – in Jaipur, Bundi, Kota – have far better collections of Rajput miniatures than the palaces of Junagarh, but Junagarh has some of the finest wall decorations of Rajasthan in the multitude of chambers in its many buildings: some decorated with glittering trees made of richly coloured chips of semi-precious stones; others with patterns of mirrors growing blue with age and so stylized as to be almost abstract; yet others with paintings of flowers and fruit as fresh and immediate as those on Austrian peasant furniture; and finally those strange murals that consist of outline paintings of flasks and bottles and other glass vessels within which one realizes that what at first sight seems to be shading in fact consists of a vast variety of tiny and exquisite monochrome miniatures – veritable minuscules – of landscapes and buildings, of animal and human encounters, all done in a style so un-Indian that one speculates whether some Bikaner prince, fascinated by the Chinese artifacts that found their way into Indian courts, did not induce into his service a painter wandering westward from Canton.

Tony and Margo, Inge and I, lingered in these romantic chambers and spun our fancies around their evocations, but the Onleys remained resolutely outside, for though the intricacies of Rajput art interested Toni, and he bought some good late reproductions of the miniatures, his preoccupation as a painter was in the great forms of the buildings and the landscape and their atmospheric relations. His theme was the walls of India and generally he followed it; he did not even put figures in his landscapes, leaving it for me to people them in words.

8. The Jewel of the Desert

The desert shifts from stone to sand and back to stone, and then to sand again, windswept dunes with a haze in the air from the blown dust. The vegetation becomes a tussocky herbage, rather like sagebrush, that barely holds the sand, and the edges of the road are blurred by the drifting dunes. The colour of the dunes shades off from yellow to mauve and rose and back to yellow. We are now almost three hundred kilometres beyond our last stop, the already remote Rajput town of Bikaner. At the end of a long, slow day of driving, our eyes are sore from the sun, our throats grated by the dust. The Ambassador, its age beginning to show, bucks and rattles on the narrow road that military convoys have chewed up, and with difficulty I scatter words on my pad, a mad shorthand which I hope I can interpret for my journal at the end of the day. Toni, sitting beside me, is unable to sketch and soaks in the colour and light with his eyes so that he can trap it all in paint once the endless fidgeting motion stops.

The desert continues, sand and stone and sand, broken by small sights that in the monotony take on the shining self-sufficiency of surrealist images. The picked-over skeleton of a bullock by the roadside, white kites prising off the last morsels. A gazelle buck staring at the car from fifteen feet off, then doing a leaping turn to bound away over the desert. A herd of camels – perhaps a hundred – guarded by two small boys as they crop the wretched scrub. A frieze-like procession of women, red clay pots balanced on their heads, walking over the sand to a village whose round storage huts look like Basuto kraals and whose little cubical houses with smoothed mud walls could have been lifted from anywhere in the Sahara. The women's shawls and wide skirts are bright red, orange, yellow – the colours of survival in the desert; they wear heavy silver anklets above their bare feet and tiers of ivory bracelets on their upper arms. Around the village, bits of roughly tilled ground, too ragged to be called fields, are being watered laboriously by men in immense red turbans from wells where oxen draw up great leather buckets; they seem to grow nothing but millet, the crop of a rainless land. No rain has fallen here, a shepherd told us in the last village, for four years.

It all seems as if it will never end. There are moments of doubt when the road shimmers into watery mirage and a man on a riding camel grows into a wandering giant and we wonder whether we are on the right road. But there is only one road over the Thar desert of Rajasthan, and eventually we top a small rise and suddenly, perhaps six kilometres away in the midst of the flatness, see the great outcrop, long and flat-topped, on which the city of Jaisalmer grows like some vast mollusc lit by the late afternoon sun, a mollusc of golden stone moulded impregnably to the rock, the spires of its nine Jain temples gleaming against the hard enamel blue of the sky.

We let out a great thirsty cry, just as the camel men must have done through the long centuries when the great caravans trod this way from Persia through Baluchistan and the desert of Sind and eastward to the Great Mogul's cities of Delhi and Agra. Surgit pulls his Sikh beard, gives a thankful salaam to the decal of Guru Nanak on the windshield, and puts his foot on the gas to speed down the long hill and land us in the spartan little tourist bungalow under the city walls, where we wet our whistles with tall bottles of Golden Eagle beer before entering the great gateway to the city.

The journey over, Surgit and Ranjit went off to find a Sikh or Hindu eating house. As we found on one occasion later on, they would sooner starve than eat Muslim food. According to our agreement, we gave them fifty rupees each for an Indian hotel, but I think they always slept in the cars and saved the money or spent it – as Surgit once remarked accusingly of Ranjit – on home-brewed liquor. The evening we got to Jaisalmer, Surgit borrowed money from Tony to buy a blanket in the handicraft store. It was cold in the car on a desert night.

It had been a tiring day, but we were all happy at the end of it, with the sense of achievement that reaching one's destination in the desert always brings, whether one travels by camel or decrepit car. And by now we had been on the road long enough to settle into an easy, accommodating relationship. Tony and Margo we had known for a long time, so that this was merely a new situation to test the firmness of our friendship. Toni Onley we had, until recently, seen mostly at art shows, and Yukiko we had met on only two or three occasions, knowing her mainly as a very elegant young woman – so elegant, indeed, that we at first wondered how well she would take to the rigours of Indian travel.

We need never have worried, for Yukiko showed herself to be a tough and adaptable traveller, enduring the exhaustions of bad cars and worse roads, stoically tramping in the Indian heat as needed, and enthusiastically eating anything that was put before her, no matter how hot a curry might be. She had a strange modesty about her talents, and it was only in Jaisalmer that we discovered that Yukiko, too, was a watercolour painter with a very clear sense of tone.

Toni and I discovered treasures of shared memories in our childhoods – his spent on the Isle of Man and mine in Shropshire – and we would spend hours comparing dialect phrases or sayings or superstitions, and building up through bandied anecdotes a deep sense of each other's past, of what had made us and so, in a sense, of what we were. At times we annoyed the others with our arsenal of local jokes and allusions.

But there were many other cross-links among us as a group. Tall, blonde Margo, now a civil servant, had studied Tibetan, as Inge had

38

done. She had also spent a year in Yukiko's native Japan. Inge and I had travelled in Japan, years before. Margo had long been involved in the Canadian Society for Asian Art. Tony Phillips, as a psychologist studying the workings of the brain, had long been interested in Asian meditational techniques, and also in Asian art. And so our interests tallied and interwove.

*   *   *

Jaisalmer is India's Ultima Thule, the last city to the northwest, less than a hundred kilometres from where the dunes merge without a break into Pakistan. It was founded in the twelfth century by Rawal Jaisal, who claimed descent through the lunar line of the Rajputs from the Yadav lineage founded by Krishna. Seeking a safe refuge in an India imperilled by Muslim invasions, Rawal Jaisal picked on the rock called Tricuta which rose like a vast stone whaleback out of the desert, and here he established the great fortress with its ninety-nine towers of sandstone encircling the mother rock.

Jaisalmer's rulers grew rich over the centuries on the tolls they charged the caravans for which the city was a welcome stopping place on the long dry journey from the Iranian highlands, and the city became populated with merchants who built the elaborate Jain temples and crammed the space within the city walls with their mansions or *havelis*, whose splendour reflected the wealth of the desert trade. Only in the present century did a light railway reach Jaisalmer from Jodhpur; the road we followed from Bikaner, such as it may have been, was built later, after the principality was incorporated into the new republic of India in 1947. There is still no airstrip serving Jaisalmer, and nothing nearer a hotel than the tourist bungalow, where big-eared desert rats roam the building at night (one of them invaded Tony's and Margo's room and was evicted with difficulty) and the only meals are curries, enormous and delicious and exceedingly hot. The bungalow was not full, and most of the guests were Indian politicians or officials. Even now, few travellers endure the journey by night train or the two days of desert driving via Bikaner which we had just completed.

Its remoteness had kept Jaisalmer less thronged than most Indian towns in the 1980s, and not only from a lack of tourists. Lack of water saved it from expanding like the other Rajasthani cities; only recently was a piped supply brought in from artesian wells among the dunes, and it is still not abundant, so that there are few new buildings in

Jaisalmer, and almost all of those are outside the great city wall around which the traffic circulates. The streets inside the gates are mostly too narrow, and on the upper parts of the rock too steep, to be more than walkways; in Jaisalmer, as in Venice, the sound of footsteps is always in one's ears because it has no rivals.

It was Arthur Erickson who first urged me to go to Jaisalmer; he had never seen a city, he said, more magically "all of a piece." All of a piece it certainly was, for the whole city had been built of the same golden stone as the walls. On the outside, it formed the massive blocks of the round bastions, in whose crenellations were posed global boulders of the same stone, to be tipped down on the heads of besiegers. On the inside, the stone was carved into the geometries that covered the walls of mansions and small houses alike and filled the lattices of the floating balconies with screens that looked like rigid lace. In every street the stone carvers had been at work, making the kind of airy, shady houses needed for the heat of the desert, and at the same time creating whole streets of architectural gems that were not deserted monuments but places where Rajput people still lived.

The princes had gone, declassed by republican India into plain citizens. But the feel of the princely past was still strong: in the temples filled with hundreds of rigid Jain images, where priests in orange robes appeared out of the incense-smelling shadows to direct one to the nearest money-chest of brassbound teak; in the bazaars of little smoky shops where spices and dyes were laid out in brilliant pyramids, and silversmiths sat weighing the heavy peasant jewellery which they sold by the gram, not by the piece, by weight rather than by artistry, which was still taken for granted; most of all, in the square high up in the citadel, with the façade of the palace – covered with balconies like rococo swallows' nests – on one side, and on the other a kind of Greek theatre of tiered stone benches from which the maharawal would hold durbars sitting on the marble throne that remained at the top level. The evening we discovered the square, an old man sat on the throne drawing elfin music out of a strange thin-toned rectangular fiddle, and on the lower benches other men played a kind of primitive chess, while little girls ran screaming in front of the palace, dragging into the sky square kites decorated with bold patterns like Kandinsky paintings.

As in most of India, it was the women of Jaisalmer who seemed to sustain their traditions most faithfully. A girl in a doorway of filigreed stone, in her brilliant mirror-inset skirt, with a gold edged mantle drawn over her head, looked exactly like a princess waiting for her lover in

Lake shrine, Jaisalmer

Jaisalmer from Bias Chhatri

Jaisalmer from Bias chhatri, India, Dec. 21/82

Jodhpur Fort

Jodhpur Fort, India, December 22 1982   onley

Evening sky, Lake Palace, Udaipur

one of the exquisite eighteenth-century miniatures that used to be painted in the courts of Rajput cities like Jaisalmer. Some of the old men also kept to past ways; one walked beside me in a brocade jacket and white jodhpurs, and told me his son was a professor of agriculture in an Ontario college. But most of them – especially the kind of men whom we bargained with in furtive upper rooms over silver jewellery and camel-bone bracelets called ivory – compromised shabbily between past and present, wearing old suit coats with muslin dhotis and white Gandhi caps instead of big, bright Rajput turbans.

Only the children in Jaisalmer had slipped entirely into the modern age. They clustered excitedly around us, anxious to touch, to hold our hands, not begging for money, but shouting, "One pen! One bonbon!" They were being prepared for the future when everything we saw around us would be changed, when the planned airport would be open and the big new hotel built on the site already marked for it. A boy greeted me in German. *"Guten Morgen, mein Herr!"* A girl excitedly warned Inge in French to have nothing to do with the two boys who talked such smooth English. These boys told us that in high school they were being taught tourism as a subject, and offered themselves as guides for the sake of practice. We accepted; they were informed and resourceful, and refused any payment except a treat of Kwality ice cream and a couple of Bic pens.

While the rest of us explored the narrow lanes, clambered on to the high walls and bargained in little holes of shops for the few authentic antiques we saw among the fakery that sweeps like an abundant flotsam over all modern India, Toni was out painting in the places where he could work best. Given his style, this meant neglecting the detail of the inner town and taking his inspiring forms from the broad masses of the fort's formidable external structure, which in the past had withstood Muslim sieges lasting for as long as twelve years. As he painted, Toni encountered two aspects of the Indian character that in his occupation could be exasperating: an unashamed curiosity about any unfamiliar activity, and a lack of any sense of another person's need for privacy. Until we reached Jaisalmer, he had painted in places where few people went, and their interest had not been oppressive. But now he found a fine view of the fort from the edge of a school playground, and suffered for an hour while the children crowded around him, shouting, jostling, standing in his light, jolting his elbow as he painted, and trying to make off with his brushes. It was the kind of annoyance he would continue to endure while he was in India. There is, in fact, only one effective way to rid oneself of such pestilential crowds of spectators. It is to declare one's intention to meditate. Privacy for spiritual ends is the only kind that is readily understood by the Indian, who spends all his life in joint households, crowded streets, and other such places where ordinary privacy, because it is impossible, becomes incomprehensible.

In Jaisalmer the desire to escape from his spectators led Toni, and us after him, to two places that gave a quite different idea of the Rajput genius for building than either the militarily serviceable masses of the fort or the elegant stone embroidery of the *havelis*.

The first was an arid hilltop whose rock ledges faced out over the scanty green patches of garden plots beneath the western walls of the city. It was the Rajput equivalent of a graveyard, except that there were no bodies buried here. Instead, a series of light and delicate domed chhatris had been built to the memory of cremated princes and noblemen. Inside the chhatris stood slabs like gravestones; on each of them the portrait of the person commemorated was carved in relief in a much starker and more archaic style than that of the miniature paintings, which are the more familiar form of the Rajput art. The latter's erotic grace, so dedicated to the celebration of the eternal instant of joy, seemed to vanish in the face of death, which was represented here not merely by the bleak style of the memorial carvings but also by the piles of ashes we found near the chhatris, from one of which Toni picked a fragment of charred bone.

The place was strangely uninhabited; we saw only a brown goat with two bounding kids and the green lizards flicking from stone to stone. Yet we had a sense of presence, as if princely spirits had found it a good place to rest between incarnations, looking out over the great fort that had resisted their enemies for eight centuries and still dominated the desert in a very different age, when Russian-made tanks clattered beneath its walls in the direction of the Pakistan border, and a bare hundred miles away, at Pokaran on the road south to Jaipur, India's first nuclear device had been exploded in 1975. From this western point, in the late afternoon just before the rapid desert nightfall, the light would grow so soft and intense that things would seem inwardly luminous, and the great fortress, ninety-nine towers and all, would change from sombre solidity into golden fantasy, from a rock into a dream.

Warfare can never have been so incessant in this region as Rajput legends suggest. If the warriors had ridden out so often in their yellow robes of abnegation to suicidal battles, there would have been neither the time nor the people to have patronized the marvellous miniature painters or to have evolved the grace of the Jaisalmer cenotaphs or the atmosphere of that even more strangely charming place, the Gadi-Sar Tank (tanks in India are artificial lakes or ponds, usually at temples). The Gadi-Sar is an odd phenomenon in a desert where rain comes once in four or five years — so rarely that small children who have never seen it are terrified when it falls — for this sheet of water, in a hollow outside the city gates, seems never to fail. In the days before piped water reached the city, the people would apparently use the tank in times of drought when the deep wells within the fort ran dry.

To reach the tank we walked under an ornate and heavily carved gateway. It was built for the pleasure of Jaisalmer's people by a courtesan named Telia, a favourite of the reigning maharawal. She had it constructed over the path by which the princely family went to perform their ceremonies at the tank, and some of them, thinking the origin of the arch might pollute them, threatened to have it pulled down. Telia learnt of their intention and, being a resourceful young woman, placed an image of Krishna in the chamber above the gate, and got the Brahmins to dedicate it as a temple. It would have been sacrilege to destroy a shrine and so Telia is remembered in Jaisalmer legends, and her gift remains as a gateway to that miraculous little lake, whose shores are lined with small, elegant temples and whose tiny artificial islands are crowned with shrines of such airiness that their reflection-doubled images have at evening a strangely Japanese-looking insubstantiality, which may have been what drew Toni and Yukiko there so often, for both of them painted when they went there. Besides, it was a tranquil place outside festival times, for most of the people there were busy making their offerings to the gods of the various temples — fruit or flowers carried on a little basket, perhaps some ghee (clarified butter) to anoint the image, or a coconut to break so that the milk flowed over it, and always, tied in the corner of a handkerchief or shawl, some small coins to be given to the priest who would chant the puja (or invocation of the god).

It was fascinating to see at this stage of our journey, as Toni painted, his experiencing self struggling with his remembering self — the painter of newly discovered Indian light emerging from the painter of northern clouds and shadows. It was obviously not an easy transition, and at one point on our second or third day in Jaisalmer, Toni could endure no longer the relentless azure of those vast and empty desert skies. So he painted in a broad swatch of heavy gunmetal cloud hanging like a doom over the yellow towers of the city. The next morning, in that town where it had not rained for so long, we woke to the smell of dampened dust as a shower licked over the battlements and vanished into the desert. Driving south from Jaisalmer that morning, into the quickly breaking sunlight, we wondered aloud at this startling vindication of Oscar Wilde's dictum that nature imitates art.

9. The Land of Death

Bikaner and Jaisalmer represent one extreme of Rajasthan, the arid heart of the Thar desert. Eastward and southward lie the chains of the Aravalli mountains, and beyond them the lake-dotted foothills of Mewar, the realm of the Sisodias, whose maharana is the highest ranked of all the Rajputs.

It is about 660 kilometres from Jaisalmer to Udaipur, the capital of Mewar, which on Canadian roads would be a comfortable day's drive. In Rajasthan it took us two exhausting days, the first by worn-out desert roads to Jodhpur, and the second by a tortuous route through the defiles of the Aravallis from Jodhpur to Udaipur.

For a good part of the first day the desert was much like that we had driven through to Jaisalmer. The light of the low morning sun made its shrubs glow as if from within like burning bushes, and created long shadows that gave gigantic status to the camels coming with their riders over the horizon toward us. There were the same Saharan villages, the same herds of camels and goats and sheep, the same clusters of artillery concealed among the dunes. Here the road workers were women, and at times swarms of them, in bright red, mirrored skirts and shawls, clustered by the roadside chipping stones with little hammers like those geologists use, while other women carried the chips in brass pans that they balanced on their heads like Greek caryatids, and dumped them to form the surface of the road – a road described in my Rajasthan guidebook as "a miracle of modern engineering."

The "miracle" was steadily shaking to pieces Surgit Singh's two old Ambassadors and at one point, in the car in which Inge and I were travelling with Tony Phillips, we heard a brittle clanking up front of the steering wheel. The radiator had broken apart and the fan was beating against it. "No problem!" said Ranjit as he tore the tail off his shirt and tried to tie the radiator back in place. In half a mile, it broke adrift again; this time Tony and Ranjit searched around, found a flat stone and a bit of old blown out tire lying by the road, and managed to wedge the radiator back in place. Stopping every now and then to adjust this precarious contrivance, we limped our way through stretches of cactus desert, areas of outcropping rock where everything – from houses to fences – was made of red stone, and plateaux of parched grassland grazed by immense flocks of sheep. Finally, we breasted a last hill and looked down from its crest on the green and tree-shaded oasis where the town of Jodhpur lies, white and rather Moorish, dotted with sugar-loaf pinnacles, like those of Le Puy but crowned with white temples instead of churches, and dominated by a tall fort, the darkest and grimmest in all Rajasthan, standing on its own bare rock above the lower town, loftier and more compact than Jaisalmer and in awkwardly sinister isolation from the life surrounding it. Ironically, despite our breakdowns and our halting progress, we reached the hotel first, for Surgit Singh, who was driving Margo, Yukiko and Toni, got so lost in the maze of narrow streets around the fortress that it took him more than an hour to find his way out.

Jodhpur was named for Rao Jodha, chief of the Rathor clan, who built the first fortress here in 1459, having been pushed out of central India by the waves of Muslim invaders, but the kingdom he ruled was originally called Marwar, the land of death, because of its terrible deserts, and the first sight of that forbidding fortress made the name seem appropriate. Of course, both Jodhpur and Marwar have other connotations. It was here that the baggy-bottomed and tight-legged riding trousers called jodhpurs were first devised for polo-playing princes, being introduced to Britain at the time of Victoria's Diamond Jubilee by Sir Pratap Singh, then the regent of the principality. The Marwaris are a clan of merchants well known in northern India; they first flourished in the region of Jodhpur under the protection of the princes, who in their turn, like medieval European kings, benefited from the money-lending capacities of men of humble caste.

Even the rulers of Jodhpur eventually became depressed by the grim gloom of their Meherangahr Fort, and created the most extraordinary of recent Rajput follies, the Umaid Bhavan Palace which Maharajah Umaid Singh built on a hillside that looks across a deep valley toward the old fort. It was started in 1928, when any perspicacious native prince should have been listening to the warning sounds of political change in India, and planned to be the biggest modern palace in Rajasthan, which it is, and the most magnificent, which it is not. Unlike Ganga Singh in Bikaner, Umaid Singh did not rely on local craftsmen working in their traditional forms. Instead, he hired Sir H.C. Lancaster, then president of the Royal Institute of British Architects, who designed him a grandiose structure of local marble and red sandstone; the few Rajput motifs were dwarfed by the immense neo-classical dome which a German visitor remarked to me should be called St. Peter-and-St. Paul, in allusion to the great cathedral domes of Rome and London, of which one was incongruously reminded. The palace was completed in 1943, and survived the débâcle of the extravagant world of Indian princedom by becoming yet another in the circuit of literally palatial Rajasthan hotels.

> Inside the palace [my Rajasthan guidebook told me] one finds oneself confronted to aristocratic setting with ambroisal and vivid decorations. The most delectable and jovial of the various portions is of course the swimming pool. The Mural Paintings with charming light arrangements, filter and water heating arrangements, in the pool are some feathers of remark.

Wandering in the chill and echoing corridors of the palace, I could detect nothing either "ambroisal" or jovial in Lancaster's sepulchrally imperial design, and if it had not been for the remarkably good tandoori sandgrouse and chicken served every night in a barbarically brilliant tent in one of the courtyards, with good folk musicians, I would have found no "feathers of remark" to convince me that we were not living in the sterile grandiosity of some midwestern American state capitol.

Shortly after our arrival, a young man came tapping at the door. He was one of the secretaries of the maharajah who, like Bikaner, still occupies a wing of his palace. He had heard of our coming, and invited us to take cocktails with him and the maharani. We gathered under the echoing dome with the other guest, a braying Oxford don, and were shepherded into the princely apartment, making our way through corridors of playing children to the parlour where Jodhpur awaited us. A tall man, dressed at casual expense in the western way, he had the kind of handsomeness one associates with popular Indian film stars and the prominent dark eyes I had already noticed in portraits of his ancestors on the walls of our room. A little later the maharani flitted in; with her manner of ethereal distress, and her traditional garb of a Rajput skirt with mantle of fine lilac and gold-threaded silk hooded over her head, she looked – like the girl in the Jaisalmer doorway – as if she had stepped out of an early eighteenth-century miniature, so conservative is women's dress in Rajasthan.

The Scotch was excellent, the curried snacks piquant, the conversation alert and interesting. Toni was encouraged to fetch his paintings, which our hosts discussed sensitively and perceptively. They were delighted of course to recognize their own fortress and to compare it with those of rival principalities, like Jaisalmer and Bikaner, but they also talked of colour and light in a way that befitted the descendants of those who had employed the great Rajput miniaturists, and the maharani called her children so that Toni could talk to them about his craft.

The maharajah recalled his days at Oxford for the benefit of the visiting academic and then, when we told him of the hospital at Kabliji, he began to talk in a way that showed how strangely the unofficial viewpoints have come together in modern India. He told us of his own concern for the villagers of his former principality. Because of its great empty spaces and few towns, rural Rajasthan has been one of the most neglected parts of India so far as medical and social services are concerned, and people in the desert regions are especially badly served. Like the other princes, Jodhpur had established a trust to prevent the wealth of his ancestors vanishing entirely into the coffers of the central government. Inevitably, the former native princes are regionalist in their sympathies, attached to their former subjects by personal loyalties and by the sense of noble obligation that in the last decades of the native states made quite a number of the rulers into model benevolent despots. So now, having dipped into his trust fund to set up a museum in the grim old fort of his forefathers, Jodhpur was planning to use the rest of it for the villagers who were once his subjects, and who have been ignored by distant governments, whether they are centred in Delhi or in Jaipur.

Talking of villages led us to talking of Mohandas Gandhi, and I was surprised to hear this former prince denounce the hypocrisy with which the leaders of the Congress Party paid nominal homage to Gandhi's fame, but in fact pursued policies that in every way contradicted his teaching. Jodhpur seemed to admire Gandhi as a kind of hero, even though he did not fight with the swords and arrows the Rajputs themselves had once used, and at the same time, he seemed to find nothing remotely heroic about the contemporary Indian Congress politician with his cant and his corruption. But he also recognized that Gandhi's most important message for independent India was that it would never flourish unless it began to regenerate its villages. The power of the Rajput princes themselves had depended on the villages where their warriors were bred, warriors who were attached to them by clan loyalties resembling those which the epics suggested existed among the Aryans of prehistoric times – the ancient and original Kshatriyas. It would be stretching things far to call Jodhpur a Gandhian maharajah, yet he was obviously near enough to the real traditions of India to understand Gandhi and his teachings rather better than most contemporary Indian political leaders.

10. Atmospherics of Udaipur

Jodhpur is the end of the real desert of Rajasthan. To reach Udaipur we travelled south on backroads through a rustic countryside still uncorrupted by the great trunk roads and full of strange and interesting places that up to now have evaded the processes of homogenization and industrialization that pass for progress in contemporary India.

In the small town of Pali, hundreds of potters were making enormous earthenware vessels with beautiful geometric slip patterns; they built them up coil by coil and beat them smooth and thin with a small wooden paddle. Despite their elegance, these were entirely utilitarian vessels used for storage, and we saw many of them standing outside the huts in the villages. Here we saw the first running river since the Jumna at Delhi, a feeble stream trickling between great gravel banks coloured bright crimson and azure and emerald by the cloths the dyers had spread out to dry, and which would be made into the vivid skirts the Rajput women wore. At Rani a large deserted fortress, an outpost of the lords of Jodhpur, enclosed the top of the hill, and little razor-backed pigs like peccaries rooted among the rubbish in the bazaar and tried to steal the apples that the fruit vendors were selling. One tiny town whose name we never learnt was a religious centre with no fewer than five temples and several hostels for pilgrims, yet here the road degenerated into a mud lane that would be impassable in the monsoon, when the ford by which we had to cross the river there would become a torrent.

A little farther on we entered a haunting landscape, shimmering under the noon sun, of small hills whose bare rockfaces had been smoothly worn as if glaciers had ground them down; they reminded one of giant reclining elephants, for the rock had a grey pachydermatous look. In a village hidden among them a large and elaborate temple had recently been entirely whitewashed into a Brobdingnagian wedding cake. In another village we stopped at a dak bungalow, thinking we might get a pot of tea brewed, as one can in similar places in South India. But only an ancient man in dhoti and shawl, grey with dirt, shambled from a shack inside the gate as we walked through the dried-up garden, and opened creaking doors onto the decrepitude within: ragged, rat-chewed mats on the dust-grey floor, worn-out rope beds with shreds of rotting mosquito nets hanging above them, chairs so obviously tottering apart that one hesitated to touch, let alone sit on them. Whether it was ever used now, and if so, by whom, we could not imagine. The old man looked at us as if we were ghosts, dream figures from some vanished past of itinerant collectors and district magistrates, but hurried to earn his baksheesh carrying buckets of water to flush the hole-in-the-floor latrines.

Eventually the first slopes of the Aravallis rose up, hog-backed and covered with low, thin, bosky forest. The narrow, twisted road clung on the valley sides above the beds of rivers where no water ran at this season but enough moisture remained to feed tiny polygonal fields of paddy and wheat. Once we stopped at a little teahouse where a boy was slapping chapatis and cooking them on an open stove. "You can have food here!" Surgit Singh exclaimed enthusiastically. "Good as a five-star hotel!" He and Ranjit went off to eat big plates of curry, and we might have joined them if we had been desperately hungry, but it was a smoke-grimed place, and the outdoor tables were coated with seasons of grease, so that none of us was very keen to risk the experiment. Instead we ate the tart little lady's-finger bananas we had bought in the last village and some Britannia biscuits Inge had prudently bought in the Jaisalmer bazaar. We did, however, drink the local "five-star" tea, since it was served in those fragile earthenware cups that in India are thrown down after one use and smashed on the ground so that the next drinker will not risk caste pollution. Their broken shards made a terracotta floor for the area outside the teahouse.

Out of these tortuous defiles, where the road rarely ran straight for a hundred yards and the sun was visible only intermittently because of the shading cliffs, we ran into a foothill region; here, after the wintry fields farther north, we rejoiced in the small farms brilliant with springing grain; the women were tall and handsome and wore wide silver armlets. We descended to an area of lakes populated by herons and cormorants, surrounded by walled green gardens and hilltops outlined with forts and watchtowers. We were entering the old state of Mewar, and crested a final low range of hills where a fortified gate guarded the pass with a notice announcing its elevation as 776 metres. A landscape of misty valleys surrounded by pointed lyrical hills out of Chinese paintings lay before us, and through it we drove into Udaipur.

Compared with Jaipur or even Jodhpur, Udaipur is a sedate city, with many gardens, gentle traffic, aristocratic buildings turned to democratic uses as part of a decentralized university. In Indian terms, it is a recent city, founded only in the sixteenth century, when Maharana Udai Singh retreated to the hills after the fortress of Chitor, original capital of Mewar, had suffered its third assault and sack, this time by Akbar's forces. Beside the lake of Pichola, which the tribal peoples of the hill country had created by building an earthen dam, Udai Singh began in 1568 the new capital which carried his name. Though the Mogul Jehangir restored Chitor to Mewar in 1616, the great fortress – so massively built that despite Akbar's artillery, much of it still survives – had such tragic memories that the maharanas never returned to it, and Udaipur remained their capital and eventually gave its name to their state.

Despite its newness, the city of Udaipur has an irregularity of planning quite unlike the quadrilateral arrangements of Sawai Jai Singh's Jaipur, and we found our way by devious and difficult routes to the great City Palace on the lakeshore, through whose gardens we reached the Bhansi Ghat, the quay where we would board the launch for the Lake Palace, the last of our series of princely hotels.

Among its many processes, travel involves the constant revision of images, and especially of the images emerging from that other process of illusory verisimilitude, photography. The Lake Palace Hotel is one of the most familiar images of India outside that country; it appears in newspapers, in advertisement brochures, in the windows of travel agencies: the vision of a white and sparkling fairy palace set in the heart of a blue, romantic lake. But the water through which we chugged in the old wooden launch from Bhansi Ghat toward the islanded palace was no more blue than the Danube, though it was green rather than brown, the green of a murky pea soup in which floating turds took the place of croutons. It stank, with that malignant sourness of the worst canal ends of Venice. I was not surprised when, later on, a waiter pointedly assured me that the freshwater fish he was serving came from a different lake. In fact, carp do survive in Pichola, for in another part of it we saw the fishermen catching them in throw nets, and one morning Surgit Singh, waking early in his car on the Ghat, saw a gigantic hamadryad cobra, well over six feet long, slither down the steps and into the water to hunt its breakfast of small fry. It was the only snake anyone of our group encountered on the whole journey through Rajasthan. There was a Jain temple near Jaisalmer where a sacred cobra lived in a hole in the temple courtyard, but though some devotee had put a saucer of milk there, we never saw him. Most Indian snakes, even poisonous ones, are shy creatures and as much afraid of man as he is of them.

As for the palace, it had grown grey from the weathering monsoons, and the stone steps onto which we leapt, with Proustian memories of *palazzi* on the Grand Canal communicating from our footsoles to our brains, had the cracked, worn feel of outlived splendour, like the great state barge of the maharanas that was moored near to the palace quay – a freshwater galleon whose gilded carvings were slowly rotting with neglect.

Still there remained the advantages Persian culture had transmitted through the Moguls to the Rajput princes who built in the seventeenth and eighteenth centuries; the Lake Palace dated from 1754, a time when the rulers of Udaipur had abandoned their early hostility to Muslim power and Muslim culture. The courtyards were shady and airy, ar-ranged for cross-draughts; we walked on winding marble paths through a charming water garden; our rooms, thanks to our travel agent being himself a Rajput princeling, had the best views over the lake.

We arrived the day before Christmas Eve; the hotel was as crowded as Bethlehem, but not with the foreigners who would have been dom-inant a few years earlier. True, the maharajah's suite was occupied by a stocky five-foot-three round-bellied Texan, travelling alone and rarely seen without his wide-brimmed stetson and expensively tooled half-boots; at meals he drank French wine at three hundred rupees a bottle. But already he seemed an antediluvian among the new guests, members of India's *très nouveau riche*, the people who in very recent years have emerged as a modern middle class, less bound by traditional inhibitions than the earlier moneyed class of hereditary merchants and money-lenders, and anxious to assume, by imitating western ways, the role which Mulk Raj Anand once defined to me as that of "the brown sahibs." Most of them were Hindus, gathering without any sense of anomaly to celebrate a Christian holiday, the men in polyester suits with no hint of native garb, the women in loudly coloured silk saris and so laden with gems that I was often reminded of Oscar Wilde's marvellous title for an uncompleted play, "The Woman Covered with Jewels." They revelled, as we did, in the ropes of lights that had been woven through the flowering vines in the courtyards, so that everyone sat in the water garden drinking execrable Indian gin with even worse tonic water, yet enjoying the magical combination of the flickering turquoise and roseate light, the musky scent on the air that hovered between jasmine and frangipani, and the intricate aural patterns of a sitar played in a room off the courtyard.

I was sick at Udaipur. The food was never very good, but the celebratory dinner on Christmas Eve prostrated me for almost a day, though I began to revive after my foodless lunchtime when Tony and Margo came in with a splendid illuminated page from the Koran which they had found in the city as a present, and I took a glass of Indian brandy that would have revivified a dying horse. I missed very little by being briefly ill, for India is a country where traditions are welcomed and absorbed without much regard for their origins. Even in areas like Rajasthan, where for the most part the British never ruled directly, Christmas is still observed as an official holiday, and that afternoon, when I felt well enough to venture into the city, we found – in this place of Hindus and Jains – that all the offices and the larger shops were closed.

Only in the narrow streets of the bazaar were the stalls open, so that we could renew the supplies of fruit we found essential to counteract the heavy spicing of most of the food we ate. Trying to extricate ourselves from a cul-de-sac created by road construction, we had to stop and let a funeral procession go by. Six men carried on their shoulders the bamboo stretcher on which the body lay, covered by the yellow cloth of death and renunciation and tied with rope like a parcel into a white translucent plastic sheet smeared with vermilion powder. About fifty men and youths padded silently behind the bier in double files. They were on their way to the burning ghat and as I realized this, I thought how seldom, except in holy places especially concerned with the rituals of death, like Benares, one sees the places where bodies are burnt. I recalled one of our very first images of India, that of the Parsee towers of silence, on top of which the vultures tear apart the bodies of the Zoroastrian dead, which were so clearly visible on their hilltops in

Bombay; the Hindu burning ghats, however, were perceptible only because of the stench that, when the wind lay in the wrong direction, would blow as a salutary reminder of mortality into the hearts of the city's most palatial buildings.

For me, and I think for Toni also, the beauties of Udaipur were mostly atmospheric; its most notable buildings were of little intrinsic interest, except for their sheer magnitude. The City Palace was immense, the largest of its kind in Rajasthan, stretching for nearly half a mile along the shore of the lake, but with its size went a brutality of mass and outline which suggested that the experience of stubborn warfare had left the Sisodia princes of Mewar obsessed with the defensible rather than the graceful. Even the interiors of the palace showed a heaviness in the handling of space, an insensitivity of sculptural outline, that contrasted with the consummate handling of architectural form and decoration at Jaisalmer, the lyrical variations of design from room to room in the old fort at Bikaner, or the intellectual geometries that emerged from the agile brain of Sawai Jai Singh in Jaipur. The rulers of Mewar may have been the most obstinately independent of the Rajputs, but their legends are all of self-destruction, of suicidal expeditions and of the mass *satis* known as *jauhar* (13,000 women burning themselves in a single mass pyre according to the least probable of the narratives). In rejecting an alliance with the Moguls, they seem also to have long rejected the Persian intellectual and aesthetic influences that so refined their fellow warriors in other areas of Rajasthan. It is significant that though there are some fine Rajput miniatures to be seen in the palace at Udaipur, the principality itself never became one of the great centres of painting.

Yet the atmospherics of Udaipur are indeed extraordinary, and the Lake Palace, set in the water between the City Palace on the eastern shore and the bosky pointed hills receding into the hazy Aravallis to the west, was the best place to observe them, so that Toni hardly moved off the island and did more painting here than in any other spot in India. All of us were happy to be back in the kind of setting of mountains and woodlands and water in which we customarily live, and though the surroundings of Udaipur looked a good deal different from those at home, they had all the elements we had missed in the desert, and most of all the magical light filtering through the moist air above the lake. The nightfalls and dawns were especially splendid. At evening a peach-coloured glow would irradiate the whole sky, turn the ochre-coloured walls of the City Palace to a glowing golden orange, and magnify the mountains as they darkened and turned flat against the sunset. At dawn, the palace would appear as a splendid black silhouette, all its imperfections darkened out, against a light-filled roseate eastern sky in which Homer's goddess seemed to have dabbled her fingers. The lake fascinated and held us and even when we took the launch to shore, it was usually to wander along the gardens on its banks and watch the women washing their clothes and hair and the fishermen casting their nets in that murky polluted water which provided such evocative mists and such shimmeringly Venetian reflections. Turner would have thrived in Udaipur.

We left the city on Boxing Day, driving north toward Agra and Delhi, on one of those cool, limpid winter mornings when India, for all its worn antiquity, shines in the low early sunlight like the most pristine country on earth. The hillsides were wide and open and scantily peopled. The lantana bushes bloomed their hot orange for miles along the roadside. The sugar cane was thin and ragged in the fields, and the cormorants stretched their wings in mimic crucifixion beside the shallow lakes. The men were muffled to the eyes in thick shawls; the women who strode erect under their water-pots wore the heavy local silver anklets between the hems of their mirrored Rajput skirts and their bare, calloused feet. An old gentleman walked out on his morning business with carved stick in one hand and, in the other, the polished brass *lotah* he would use in his ablutions. Pack camels padded the road with great burdens of straw or reeds jutting vastly on each side of them.

An hour or so out of Udaipur, near the village of Kankroli, we began to see women in brilliant orange mantles, glittering with stars of silver or gold braid, hurrying along the road. In a little while we were held up by white-clad marshals with red flags and whistles; a procession was about to start off. There was no band, no singers; the marchers walked silently and with pride under their banners inscribed in Rajasthani: first the schoolchildren, all neatly dressed European-style, in shirts and shorts, blouses and skirts; then the women in their bright, traditional garb, some of them carrying babies; finally the men and the older boys.

"Jaini peoples," commented Surgit Singh, who could read their banners, and indeed, immediately after we had passed this procession of laymen, we encountered the real Jain pilgrims, the renunciates clad entirely in spotless white, with white half-masks covering their mouths and noses to prevent their destroying minute organisms by breathing them in, and bundles wrapped in white cloths balanced on their heads. "So many ladies, some old men," said Surgit, with his soft giggle that always implied superiority to all people who were not Sikhs. There were, indeed, only three or four old men, yet they were the most devout pilgrims of all; they carried little besoms and gently swept the road before their feet so that they would not step on any worms or insects that happened to be there.

We thought it strange that in leaving Rajasthan, the land of warrior kings, the last people we saw should have been these men and women of peace and – more than ordinary peace – of the total nonviolence that was preached by Mahavira, the great contemporary of Buddha and founder of the Jain religion, one of the philosophic ancestors of Gandhi. The dry land through which they were walking glistened with mica as if it had been strewn with diamonds.

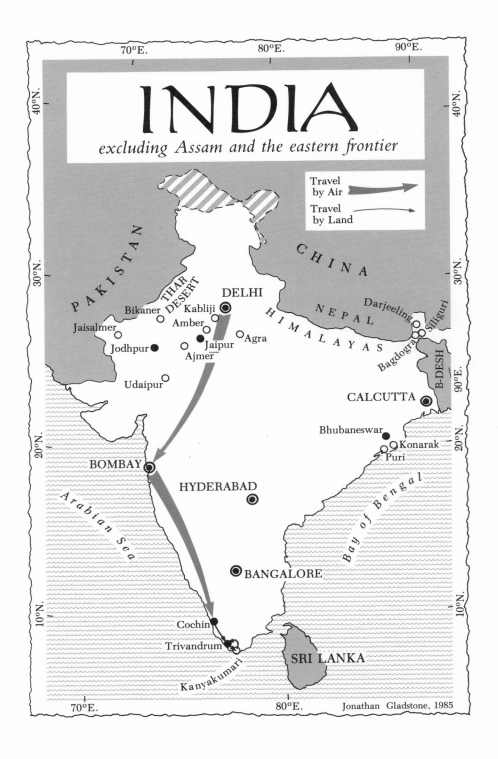

Lake Fort, Udaipur

Lake Fort, Udaipur, India, December 24 1982

Fatehpur Sikri

Fatehpur Sikri, India December 28 1982   onley

Fatehpur Sikri

Fatehpur Sikri. India. December 23. 1982   onley

Lodi Tombs, Delhi

Lodi tombs. Delhi, India. December 30 1982

III

KERALA

December 31, 1982 – January 7, 1983

11. Slow Plane to Cochin

It is an extraordinary transition from the climatic extremities of Rajasthan – cold winters anticipating burning summers – and its terrestrial rigours of desert and dry mountain, to the green and damp of Kerala, that tropical province in the far south of India where the rain forests march down the Western Ghats to merge into the vast palm groves that surround the endless coastal lagoons and fringe the broad beaches facing the Arabian Sea. But in our case it was hardly an abrupt transition, for it took us the whole of New Year's Eve to get from Delhi to Cochin by air, and most of the time was spent in aimless waiting. The weather had been cold in Delhi and all of North India, and every morning thick fog had drifted up from the Jumna to lie until ten or eleven o'clock over the runways at Palam Airport. Planes were late leaving Delhi and, since the internal service known as Indian Airlines is highly centralized, this meant that, by domino effect, planes were late over the whole country and latest of all at the extremities.

We stood for hours in the dense queue at Palam, waiting to book in on the plane to Bombay, where we had to change for Cochin. At last a porter anxious to earn an extra ten rupees told us that an earlier plane to Bombay, not quite so delayed as ours, had a few seats unfilled. We happily boarded it – Toni and Yukiko, Inge and I. Margo and Tony had left us to return to Vancouver after a splendid party in Patwant Singh's house, with painters and journalists, civil servants and diplomats and, most pleasant and unexpected for me, the poet John Smith who had been my literary agent in London for a quarter of a century until his retirement and, travelling through India, had called on Patwant, another of his clients. John and I spent most of that evening talking of old writer friends, and sadly recognizing that we must class ourselves as survivors, so many of them were dead.

Getting on the earlier plane was an empty triumph, for as soon as it was ready to leave the captain announced that there would be a delay because one passenger was missing. We stayed an hour on the tarmac while the crew and the passengers argued with growing excitement. It appeared that after booking in, the passenger had disappeared, but his luggage had been brought on board. It was a time of tension in Delhi, for the Khalistan separatists who wish to turn the Punjab into an independent state had already performed acts of sabotage and threatened others; to herald the New Year by blowing up a whole planeload of passengers was the kind of outrageous gesture they might be expected to perpetrate.

Once that idea had begun to catch on, the passengers grew even more agitated. It was no longer a matter of missed connections. If the bomb was on the plane it might go off at any moment. Some people shouted out, demanding that the luggage be unloaded. Others pushed their way toward the open door to be near it in case of panic. And then at last, perhaps because they feared the likelihood of a riot on the plane more than the possibility of a bomb in the hold, the airline officials suddenly announced that the matter had been sorted out. No straggling passenger ever came on board. Had he existed except as an error in the mind of some counter clerk? We were never told.

But we need not have been anxious about our connection. By the time we reached Bombay, the all-India delays had built up, and we spent more hours pursuing the porters who had grabbed our luggage, and standing in sluggish queues to confirm our bookings yet again; on Indian Airlines, neither passengers nor luggage are automatically booked to their final destinations, so that every time one changes planes, the process must be repeated. Then there was the paranoiac Indian security check, with the officer probing in particular suspicion through Toni's patent painting kit, and finally more hours spent sweltering in a packed waiting room where the ceiling fans flapped slowly and we had to squat against the walls because all the seats were full, tut-tutting as we read the revelations on child labour, prostitution and caste murders among students which the news magazines in English – *India Today, The Week, Delhi Recorder* – were publishing with the zest of Victorian moral crusaders as spice for the depressing news of the political corruption that is almost epidemic in modern India.

At four o'clock, instead of one, our plane finally took off for Cochin, winging down over the treacherous reefs of the Konkan coast and the arid land of northern Malabar, until the coconut groves lay in a dense green sea below us, and the white towers of the Syrian churches stood out like archaic lighthouses as they gleamed in the last light of the falling sun. That sun was dipping behind the palm-fringed atolls which close in Cochin Harbour when we put down at the airport on Willingdon Island.

Most of our fellow passengers were Keralans returning from periods of work in the states of the Persian Gulf. In the 1960s, when I first knew it, Kerala was one of the most politically turbulent parts of India because of high education (double the general Indian literacy rate) combined with widespread poverty and unemployment. In 1957 it had become the first region in the world freely to elect a Communist government, though even as Communists the Keralans turned out to be like no others. The government was formed entirely of Nambudiri Brahmins, the highest Indian sub-caste, and Syrian Christians, members of the top-ranking church, with not a single low-caste man among them; Nambudiripad, the Chief Minister (equivalent to a Canadian provincial premier), consulted his astrologer every morning before he went into cabinet meetings.

Temporarily at least, the chance of a renewed Communist government was removed in the 1970s when Keralans found that better education favoured them for employment in the oil states of the Gulf. They went there in their thousands and returned, in local terms, as wealthy men.

At Cochin, after our plane had landed, the passengers waited in noisy restiveness until the luggage began to appear, and then they descended on it in a shouting, jostling mob, dragging away ancient cabin trunks, and ant-proof tin boxes, and cardboard packing cases, and enormous suitcases tied up with red and orange plastic rope, and expensive electronic equipment of every kind. In the midst of this turmoil came the announcement that half the luggage was being taken to another hall, and we had to join the stampede to the far end of the airport building, where at last we completed the tally of our possessions and found a taxi to take us to the Malabar Hotel, the old hostelry that looks out over the harbour toward the sunset, where Inge and I had stayed on our earlier visits in 1961 and over the long winter of 1965-66 when we lived there to prepare my book on Kerala.

In spite of reassuring telegrams we had received in Delhi, the Malabar was crammed to its Dutch-tiled roofs with tea planters who had come down from the Ghats for a New Year's binge, and we had to go on a long drive over the causeways to the town of Ernakulum on the other side of the harbour, where we found rooms in a hotel frequented by Australian seamen and white whores who roamed the corridors tapping on doors and talking into keyholes.

The hotel was a new concrete building, already soiled and unkempt. The clothes on our bed had been messily slept in, and we had to put on the show of fury which Inge and I call the "sahib game" to get clean sheets. The dining room had been taken over for a New Year's celebration, and we had to eat via room service. But almost nothing on the menu was available because the cooks were looking after the New Year's party; all we could get were omelettes, and they arrived an hour late and cold, with the sickening taste of tepid coconut oil. Then, since the establishment stood on the harbour-front road, we endured the new year being born: the shouting in the streets; the banging of whole volleys of firecrackers; the blaring of car and motor-bike horns, with the ships' foghorns providing a booming ground-bass; and from two floors below, the thud and throb of the band rising to the crescendo of "Auld Lang Syne." Thirty-six years after independence, Indians have remained astonishingly attached to the minor rituals of the British Raj.

On rising next morning, we saw the rough road below the window, its broken, dusty sidewalks lined with sleazy small hotels and gloomy seamen's bars, on the other side of it an abandoned construction site with reinforcing bars sticking out of the water that had seeped in, and beyond that the forest of cranes on Willingdon Island which showed how large a port Cochin had become since last we were here. Yet the old wooden ferry we had used so often still chugged over the harbour with the people crowded under its tattered canvas awnings; and country craft with upturned prows and sterns and matting sails still plied among the moored freighters; and in the shallows the fishermen still flitted in their dugout canoes, casting their nets for small fishes.

Down in the lobby an Australian who looked like a boatswain was arguing with an Anglo-Indian tart, and a blond boy in tight shorts was pulling him away. "Come on, Dave! Come on, Dave!" he kept on whining; "we'll never make it!" With the taste of last night's cold omelette in my mind if not on my palate, I remembered a modest hotel in a garden street of Ernakulum where we had eaten dinner once, nearly twenty years before. And the International was still there – quiet, spotlessly clean, inexpensive – and run by a family of kindly Syrian Christians. They welcomed us, immediately recognized our anxiety over travel agents being closed on New Year's Day, and set about making the arrangements we needed for the rest of our time in Kerala, booking our hotel at Trivandrum, the capital, where we intended to go next, arranging a car to take us south, fixing up a boat the next day so that we could sail into the waterways north of Cochin where Toni wanted to start painting, and finding a driver for our time in Cochin. He was a very black little man with an image of the Virgin as Queen of the Heavens swinging on his windshield. His name was, almost predictably in this stronghold of Latin Catholics, Joseph, and he immediately showed his ingenuity by taking us on that "dry" day to a building where we passed a handful of rupees through a small hole in a steel shutter and received a bottle of McDowell's Premium whisky, the best of the Indian distillations.

12. The Ships of the Yavanas

There had been rioting in Kerala – we heard about it from the steward on the plane coming south – and that afternoon, when we drove around the great sickle of the harbour toward Fort Cochin on the far western side, we saw the squads of khaki-uniformed, helmeted riot police in the narrow streets of Mattancheri, and a few charred shop fronts which the rioters had burned and looted. The newspapers, perhaps afraid of inflaming passions, had made little attempt to explain the disturbances, but talking to our driver and to some young men we met at the Dutch Palace, I gathered it was the Muslims who had rioted because the police, who are mainly Hindus, had fired on an Islamic procession in the coir-making town of Alleppey just south of Cochin.

To me, with my memories of the Malabar coast, it was disturbing news. Kerala has long been the model region of India in terms of communal peace, where the various ancient religious groups – Hindus and Christians, Muslims and Jews – have lived together in an astonishing degree of harmony, particularly when one considers how riven internally the various communities are, the Hindus divided into more castes and sub-castes than anywhere else in India (more than four hundred, according to my count), the Christians into a dozen mutually contemptuous churches, from the Syrians and the Chaldeans down to the Latins (despised because they are descended from the low-caste fishermen St Francis Xavier converted), and even the Jews – split between the White Jews and the Black Jews who are buried on different sides of the great wall they built through the heart of their Sephardic cemetery. To describe this paradoxical situation of social harmony combined with extreme division, one might well adapt Robert Frost and

and the state of Israel was founded. Then most of the Black Jews, who were mainly poor working people, departed. The majority of White Jews, who had money they could not take out of India, stayed with their wealth, and though the young have now scattered in the big cities, still a remnant remains in Jewtown: older, ivory-skinned men and women with a tendency to reddish hair.

It was obvious that, since we had mingled with them two decades ago, the cohesion as well as the numbers of the Cochin Jews had declined. The Paradesi Synagogue, dating from the later sixteenth century, is said to be the oldest in the Commonwealth; with its ancient Canton tiles and its hanging lamps of old roseate glass, its shining brass enclosures and the ark containing the scriptures in their splendid gold- and silver-crowned cases given by princes and governors, it is a small gem of a building. But there is no longer a rabbi, and though it was sabbath, the attendant I remembered from the past was showing visitors around and exhibiting the copper plates engraved in Malayalam script that recorded the land grant by a tenth-century Keralan king to a Jewish chieftain, Joseph Rabban.

Going north to Fort Cochin, from which Portuguese, Dutch and British successively maintained their suzerainty over the native princes of the Malabar coast, we followed lanes lined by Dutch warehouses, wide-balconied and heavy-roofed; through the gaps between them, we saw the country craft with their woven cane awnings moored thickly in front of the wharfs. And then we came to the big, open channel leading from the south into Cochin harbour, with the freighters sailing in past the extraordinary spidery structures of the cantilevered dip nets whose combination of beams and spars, ropes and pulleys, gave them the appearance of archaic war machines, particularly when arranged as they were at Fort Cochin, in long lines on the foreshore. They are called Chinese nets, because their originals were introduced by Canton traders who came in the great commercial era of the Ming dynasty and left the shards of their pottery thickly strewn among the great beaches of Quilon to the south of Cochin, which was their main destination. Long before then, in the days of Cleopatra, the Greek ships had sailed here from Alexandria and left a memory in the epic poems of the ancient Tamil kings: "Agitating the white foam, the beautifully built ships of the Yavanas came with gold and returned with pepper."

But the oldest surviving relics at Fort Cochin were of the Portuguese, and especially the old church of St Francis, built originally in 1503 by Catholic friars and taken over by successive waves of

Protestantism – the Dutch Reform Church and then English Low Church Anglicanism – which replaced any Iberian splendour that might originally have existed with a dour northern austerity, so that the interior is now as bleak as any church in one of those North Sea ports from which many of the later rulers came. But some of the dead do not allow themselves to be forgotten. Vasco da Gama died in Cochin and a low brass rail still marks out the area of his grave on the church floor, even though the bones of the navigator were taken to Lisbon more than four hundred years ago.

As we were looking at the temporary resting place of that rather repulsive personification of the Sword-and-Cross type of imperialism, the old verger who had been hovering expectantly around us signalled from the vestry door. He opened a tall cupboard and pulled out big, crumbling volumes which were the Dutch and British records of baptisms and burials: long-forgotten sea captains and women dying young in childbirth and ensigns in their teens rotting away with gangrene and children expiring by the score from cholera in an age of primitive medicine – and then a fragile bundle of ancient palm leaves that in fine and fading Malayalam script recorded the original grant of the land for the church by the sixteenth-century ruler of Cochin, whom the Portuguese overawed with their cannon and their ruthlessness. The whole tragic cycle of European intrusion into India was suddenly encapsulated in the little pile of documents on the worm-eaten Victorian desk before us.

We chose a different way back from the narrow lanes between the buildings in Mattancheri – a road that swung to the seaward side of the peninsula and went past the spacious British-era mansions, tropical Palladian in style, where the remaining merchant notables of Cochin live. Beyond, there were naval yards guarded by cannon of the Wellingtonian age, and then coconut groves under whose ubiquitous shade small houses of palm leaf were nestling in green and flowery gardens rather like those of Malay kampongs.

We came finally to a broad, open space, a kind of common, where people were gathering. A communist flag flew in one corner and an orator had gathered an audience, but he did not seem to be the main focus of the gathering. An unbroken stream of people was pouring into the space from the south, and as we continued along, we found the lanes jammed with a great straggling concourse that extended for several miles and sometimes became so thick that we had to stop our car while the walkers flowed on either side of us. It was a remarkable manifestation of the crowding of Kerala, the most densely populated state of India.

They were mostly younger folk, the men in white or light-coloured shirts and trousers, the women in luminously brilliant saris and skirts that wonderfully set off the beauty of their dark Malayali skin and large liquid eyes and black hair. All of them, in contrast to the crowds of North India, were spotlessly clean, and we all felt we had seldom seen so many fine-looking people gathered in a single place.

Remembering the riots of a few days before, we also felt a little apprehensive at being engulfed in this river of people that seemed to be moving on with a strong, set purpose, but in fact all we received were smiles and, from many of them, New Year's greetings in English. As experience had taught us in the past, there is great good will toward strangers in Kerala, perhaps because of the wandering traders and travellers who have been passing through the land for two thousand years. Inge and I recalled the time, long ago in Trichur, north of Cochin, when we were caught in a car in the middle of a riot over the lack of rice; it was a riot about culture rather than shortage, for there was plenty of inexpensive wheat in Kerala at the time, but this was a north Indian food the Malayalis despise, and they wanted nothing but rice. The young rioters had advanced menacingly upon us, but as soon as one of their leaders shouted, "Stop! They are foreigners! They have nothing to do with our troubles!" they fell away, cheered us, and went off to smash windows, set fire to a stadium, rough up a visiting government minister, and be beaten by the long bamboo *lathis* with iron tips that are wielded by Indian police.

Receptiveness to foreigners and to foreign religions has not made the Keralans entirely forgetful of their traditions, yet when we sought a performance of Kathakali, the ancient local form of dance drama, we found it harder to locate than twenty years before. Though this was the dance season, no dramas were being staged in the temple yards as they had been on our earlier visits, and all we could find was a performance for the benefit of visitors that was being put on in a barnlike palm-leaf building in one of Ernakulum's parks.

Compared with the interminable and highly adorned performances we remembered – performances that would go on all night at the temples, watched by crowds seated on the ground in the light of flaming oil lamps, with splendid interludes of virtuoso drumming – this was a worse than inadequate occasion. It began with a painfully didactic artificiality as a young woman lectured us in virtually incomprehensible

67

English while a male dancer, wearing the brilliant mask that is actually built freshly onto the face for each performance out of a paste of lime and rice flour, demonstrated the movements that display thought and emotion, the intricate *mudras* of hand and eye and head, and the appropriate steps made with those calloused and strangely prehensile-looking feet that the Kathakali dancer develops from the practice of balancing himself as he dances on the edge of his downturned foot. The soles of the dancer's feet are turned toward each other, a curious kind of distortion that adds a mildly acrobatic quality to the performance when the dancer moves about the stage, and thus rather contrasts with the delicate gestures of eye and hand. To achieve this ability, and to acquire a knowledge of the *mudras*, and of the many parts in Kathakali, the dancer goes through a rigorous eight years of training in classrooms that are called *kalaris* after the schools where the ancient Nairs were taught their military arts and which are just as rigorous in their training. In the past, in fact, the arts of war and peace were so closely linked that some of the most famous Kathakali dancers of the eighteenth century were also notable warriors.

Only at the end of the show, in a fragment of a traditional Kathakali drama based on the *Ramayana*, could this particular dancer show his virtuosity of mime and motion, and the drummer and the narrator, who chanted the story to the tune of clashing cymbals, demonstrate the skills acquired in many years of practice, for both were old men. Few younger men have the kind of memory needed to become a narrator, or Ponnani, in the Kathakali tradition. For the Ponnani has to know by heart the elaborate narratives of dozens of dramas written by Malayali poets for Kathakali performances over the centuries; he also acts as producer of the drama, assigning the roles to the dancers according to his knowledge of their abilities; and by his singing, he sets the pace of the performance. In its own way, it is as exacting a role as that of the dancer.

The female role – Rama's queen Sita – was unfortunately played by a woman who was plump and poorly trained, and so the whole tone of the performance, the necessary and complex artificiality of Kathakali, where all roles are traditionally played by men of the warrior caste, was destroyed. It was like putting a woman in one of those delicate young girl roles in the Kabuki drama which one sees so movingly played by aging male actors.

Even today, one cannot imagine such a breach of dramatic tradition in Japan, and the fact that it can and does happen in India shows how much the traditional arts have lost their essential character there in recent years. This, I think, is because they have been detached from the religious contexts to which they belong, those of temples and sacred compounds, and have been taken over by groups whose aim is to preserve culture rather than liturgy, and who are therefore willing to make adaptations that increasingly divorce the dance from its source of inspiration. Bharat Natyam, the form originally used by the deva-dasis, who combined the role of dancers for the gods with that of sacred prostitutes, is now detached from both the carnal and the spiritual aspects of the original holy vocation. It has become rather like putting on the Tridentine mass as a show in a provincial repertory theatre.

What we saw in that wretched barn in Ernakulum, in the smell of cheap joss sticks, with the clicking and flashing of tourists' cameras behind us, was a parody of a noble dramatic and epic tradition.

13. Malabar Waters

The waterways entwine in a great network along the whole coastal region of Kerala. Canals and backwaters thread for hundreds of miles inland, though even a helicopter would be unable to map them, so well concealed they are by the overhanging coconut palms. And along the coast the wide saltwater channels flow between great, low islands and small atolls, all created in the everlasting piling of sand by the tides of the Arabian Sea. These waterways have been the arteries of Kerala's long and varied commercial life; from the earliest days of the region's history, its pepper and ginger, cardamom and cloves, copra and coir, and more recently its tea and coffee, rubber and tapioca, have come down from the lush groves and gardens and plantations of the interior in long wooden country craft or *wallams*, sewn together with coconut fibres, to the wharfs and factories on the seacoast.

Our boat was waiting when we went down to the pier at Ernakulum, a launch of the same look and vintage as the *African Queen*, with solidly planked sides, hard benches and a wooden awning, a sturdy chuffing engine built in the 1930s, and a barefooted crew of skipper, engineer and deckhand who had perhaps a hundred words of English among them, though that was enough, with signs and the quickness of the Malayali mind, for us to get along very well. They were all Christians and, I gathered, belonged to the Syrian rite of the Catholic church.

These were people of the Syrian church who were forcibly converted by the Portuguese in the sixteenth century and did not rejoin their own church but kept its distinctive rituals. The skipper was a bright, wiry man of some education who knew the coastal inlets and islands as a fish knows its water and had an idea what visitors expected to find. The engineer, a fat quiet smiler of a man, most of the time sat watching his engine as if it were a beloved animal and smoking endless beedies, the little handmade cigarettes of rank tobacco that many Indians relish. The deckhand was a shy adolescent who watched Yukiko and Inge with a kind of goggling interest that might have betokened either curiosity or admiration; he was always there to take our hands when we went ashore.

Feeling there should be some kind of target, we had set our destination at Cranganore, well north of Cochin, which is a kind of node of Keralan history. There, St Thomas is said to have made his first landing; there, the Cochin Jews originally settled; there stands the oldest mosque in India, a modest little square building, with neither a dome nor a minaret, which Inge and I remembered from our earlier visits. But really we had come so that Toni could paint, and when the skipper, entering intelligently into our problems, remarked that we would probably find more interesting scenes in the narrow waterways linking the wide main channels, we abandoned our historical pieties and drifted with muted engines into the world of the island people whose fishermen ancestors St Francis Xavier converted nearly five centuries ago, thereby assuring, since one's caste is remembered even if one abandons the Hindu faith, that the Roman Catholics – or the Latins as they are called on the Malabar Coast – should remain forever, in social terms at least, at the bottom of the elaborately tiered ecclesiastical totem pole, as they would have remained at the bottom of the ladder of caste if they had not been converted. Social prejudices last long and die hard in India.

It was a Sunday, but in these Christian islands, with their new concrete churches stridently painted in Art Deco styles so that they looked like structures of cheap and gaudy sugar candy, that did not seem to diminish the amount of activity, mostly on and in the water. Some men were operating the pulleys and counterweights that raised and lowered their big Chinese dip-nets that jutted out from the shores of the channels. The catches were never great, and the crows would take a tithe by leaping into the nets before the fishermen could clear them, yet we could see nothing being done to discourage these insolent pests; indeed, they competed with the splendidly coloured mahogany-backed Brahminy kites for rulership of the water. Other men were up to their waists in the shallows, dragging in small seines, and yet others went in dugout canoes along the lines of stakes thrust into the bottom to check the captive lines. On each stake perched a gleaming white tern which would circle away when the fishermen approached and then return. Some of the men in canoes were hauling in baited lines which, the boatmen told us, were used for catching crab, and finally there were those who with a quick flick of the hand made their throw-nets spread out wide to catch anything that might be walking on the bottom. A couple of the throw-net fishermen begged a tow from us; they were young and gaunt, with almost black skins, clad only in loincloths and wide coolie hats made of woven palm leaf to shade their eyes and necks from the intense light reflected from the water. As they drifted along-side, one of the men lifted a mat to show their catch, kept in the bilge water at the bottom of the canoe: there was a medium-sized crayfish, about a dozen large prawns, a small crab and a few tiny fishes. Though there did not seem much profit in the fisherman's calling here, many still followed it.

Everywhere, as we chugged along, we could see the thatch or tile roofs of houses built either of wood or of intricately woven palm leaf, hidden among a lush and monotonous vegetation; palm trees always leant far out over the water at precarious angles, mangroves marched into the shallows in dense, dark cohorts, and rare splashes of colour, from hibiscus or bougainvillea, broke the verdant walls of the shore-side bushes. The only cultivation in evidence was of coconuts, bananas, and a few patches of tapioca, its great leaves like hands with spread fingers; the only native industries that seemed to rival fishing were coir- and copra-making and brick-making. Coir and copra are both derived from the coconut; coir is the fibre from the outer husk which is spun into ropes and woven into matting, and copra is the dried flesh of the nut from which coconut oil and other products are obtained. Here and there in the shallows the husks lay rotting and stinking, and women were cudgelling the more nauseatingly decayed ones to separate the fibres. The flesh of the nuts, halved into white cups, lay drying in the sun outside the houses.

Around almost every turn in the channel, we would see a little brickworks with the grey lines of bricks standing to dry before they were built up for firing in structures like long, miniature Peruvian pyramids under tall, palm-leaf roofs that would protect them in wet weather. Firing holes were left as the structure was built, trapezoid in shape and corbelled to support the upper mass, and after the space inside the pile had been filled with coconut trunks cut into logs, the fire was lit, the holes were filled, and the heat within slowly baked the bricks as the smoke seeped up through the cracks and billowed out under the overhanging shelter. Whatever clay may have existed in the islands must have been exhausted long ago, for we met country craft being poled along to supply the kilns, craft so heavily loaded that the clay itself was moulded to create extra freeboard and save the craft from being swamped. Malayali watermen are expert at loading these boats to the very edge of submersion.

As we drifted along, the dense human and avian population of the islands ensured that there was always something to catch the eye: the intense blue flash of a diving kingfisher or a canoe load of brightly clad people waving as they paddled from island to island on Sunday visits; a couple of paddy birds stepping stealthily through the shallows like small bitterns; two naked little boys paddling a miniature dugout of their own with skill and sureness. More and more scenes recalled past visits in Kerala, and I felt a great surge of affection for this region we had spent such a strenuous time exploring nearly two decades ago.

I remembered how Inge and I had arrived in the fall of 1965 to write a book on Kerala (it eventually appeared as *Kerala: A Portrait of the Malabar Coast*) with only three introductions, and how the Malayalis, whose interest in strangers is only exceeded by their interest in themselves, had entered into my enquiry with such spirit and enthusiasm and hospitality that my three original acquaintances multiplied like the loaves and fishes of the Bible until at the end of my three months, I must have talked at length to at least three hundred people and established a fund of information and insights that enabled me to bring into a coherent pattern the extraordinary mixture of cultures and traditions which make Kerala unique even in India.

People and places flashed into my mind as we drifted through the green shadows. The former Maharajah of Travancore, a soft-spoken and gentle ex-absolute monarch whose dress of shirt and waistcloth differed from that of ordinary Malayalis only in being of finer cotton; his mother, a living embodiment of Keralan matriarchy, sat there as we discussed the stages in which he surrendered his power to liberated India. And, on the balcony of a shabby Trivandrum house, the stuttering Marxist leader, E.M.S. Nambudiripad, another man in plain garb who once headed Kerala's freely elected Communist government.

Malabar Backwaters, Kerala

malabar backwaters, Kerala, india, January 1983

Sri Padmanabhaswamy Temple, Trivandrum, Kerala

Temple, Nandidrug, near Bangalore

Sun Temple (Black Pagoda), Konarak, Orissa

Sun Temple (Black Pagoda) Konarak, Orissa, India, January 11 1985

Being a high Brahmin as well as a Marxist, he consulted an astrologer before cabinet meetings, and when we met, he talked with most un-communist delight about the incorrigible individualism of the people of Kerala. Out in an old house among the palm groves of Allepey, sad William Bandey, the last of the local sahibs, who managed a failing coir factory and communed with a ghostly family of missionary children who died of cholera one night in 1835. Samuel Koder, one of the last of the Cochin Jews, who invited us to sabbath dinner in his great merchant's house, filled with Portuguese furniture, at Fort Cochin, and chanted the prayers in an old Sephardic Hebrew that would not be understood in Israel. A purple-robed Latin Catholic bishop at an illegal cocktail party in the dry town of Calicut who delegated his secretary to take us up to a mission in the High Ranges of Wynad where the Jesuits gathered the tribes from the jungle to dance for us to the tune of monkey skin drums and display their powerful longbows whose steel-tipped arrows could kill tigers. And the poor farmers in a remote village where we had gone to find an ancient temple, carved out of a giant boulder in the middle of the rice paddies. They sent a man cycling three miles to get a teacher who knew English so that the old priest could tell us the legend of Murugan, the pre-Hindu god of the place, and then they garlanded us with frangipani and ginger flowers and fed us fresh coconuts and savoury rice cakes. No wonder, as we left Sultan's Battery, our last town in Kerala, and Hajji Moussa, the leading Muslim merchant, accompanied us to the Karnataka border with a gift of coffee and pepper from his own plantation, Inge had said, "A sweet land we're leaving!"

We were back in the sweet land and as we sailed on through the backwaters we would see small settlements with wharfs where ferry-boats with names like *Theresa Baby* or *Mary Girl* would be moored and a ramshackle bus would be starting off down the sand roads. Once we went ashore at a jetty where there was a little clapboard store at the end; men sat playing cards and drinking palm toddy that looked like muddy water, and we bought sharp-flavoured little island bananas and a pineapple as big as a rugby ball, cut ripe and juicy from the plant. The storekeeper offered us toddy. Inge had never liked it and Toni and Yukiko were put off by its unappetizing appearance, but I accepted a glass to renew a flavour I had first experienced in these backwaters. It was tart and yeasty, already beginning to ferment, and as I toasted the storekeeper I remarked that the juice must have been gathered from the crown of the coconut palm five or six hours ago at dawn. He laughed, and clapped me on the arm. "You been here before," he said as he walked us back to the boat.

But most often we stopped to moor in the shade, tying up to the posts that stick up everywhere in the channels, much as they do in Venice, while Toni would work out the patterns given him by the dominance of vegetation green and sky-sea blue (a colour range surprisingly less variant than that offered by the desert with its shifts and shadows) and by the man-made shapes – the strong dark curves of the country craft and the shapes of the Kerala roofs with their bleached terracotta colour, which have such a Japanese look, yet in fact derive partly from a kind of Dutch tiled roof, to be found on seashores all over the East from Cochin and Colombo to Malacca and Jogjakarata, and partly from the native tipped-eaved palm-leaf huts in which so many of the Malayalis still live, in the islands as well as on the mainland.

Sitting in a corner of the boat, painting quickly with his big Japanese brush, a sun hat pulled down over his bearded face, Toni looked like a true heir to all the Victorian painters who had wandered India sketching *en plein air*, and I was reminded that just over a hundred years ago Edward Lear had passed this way, painting in the lagoons from little boats the sketches from which he made the landscapes that earned his living; the nonsense rhymes and comic drawings that accompanied them had been the light relief in the life of a hard-working artist.

Most of the time we were left in peace, except when passing boats would veer close to us out of curiosity and their occupants shout a greeting and go on their way. But once, when we drew right in, close to the shore, there were more houses hidden among the trees than we had expected and immediately, as happens in India, a crowd of spectators formed: little children whose large Byzantine eyes had been emphasized by kohl, bare-torsoed youths and handsome girls in white blouses and school skirts, men and women, one of whom wore a splendid pair of massive gold earrings. They clustered along the shore, leaning into the boat, pointing and talking excitedly. And soon Toni's audience was not entirely on shore. A canoe paddled by three young women with bright eyes and bright saris came floating by; a few minutes later they paddled gently back, their dugout loaded to the gunwales with five of their equally pretty friends. Toni painted away silently and happily; it was a less intrusive audience than he had encountered in many other places; nobody was trying to steal his brushes. Inge and Yukiko stepped on shore and gave some sweets to the dark-eyed children; some of the young women gently touched them.

The toddy was sneaking up on me, and while all this was going on I lay down to doze on one of the benches of the boat, but every now and then, from the group on the shore, I heard in the midst of their excited Malayáli chatter, the long-drawn-out exclamation, "Beautiful!" It was the only English word I heard them using, and they obviously picked it with Keralan courtesy so that their visitors should be pleased. Toni was. "I'd much sooner have them as an audience," he remarked, "than the Canadian art critics. They look at my work; the critics talk about nothing but the money I make."

14. Pepper for Roman Gold

Long ago, in the first century of our era, when the Jews and Christians came to the Malabar Coast in the ships of Greek mariners, Kerala was a united kingdom. Then, as now, the women enjoyed extraordinary power in a matrilineal society, and the snake-worshipping Nair warriors kept the frontier on the Western Ghats against the imperially minded Chola and Pandya rulers of Tamilnad. But during the period that corresponds to the European Middle Ages, the kingdom of Kerala disintegrated under Tamil pressure, and when its people regained their freedom from external rule, there was no longer one king, but a number of local princes, among whom the Zamorin of Calicut in the north and the kings of Cochin halfway down the Malabar coastline and of Travancore even farther south, emerged as the dominant figures, each of them playing his precarious game of defence and diplomacy combined, as the European intruders appeared from the sea, and the Muslims came down from the plateaux of Mysore to invade the domain of the Zamorin. In that last struggle the East India Company eventually intervened, saving Calicut from its Islamic invaders, but only at the price of its being subjected entirely to British rule; the last vestige of the Zamorin's power was taken away from him in 1800.

Cochin and Travancore survived as autonomous principalities, with all their local idiosyncrasies, under the aegis of the Raj until India became independent in 1947 and the native states were abolished. For a number of reasons, these were among the most advanced areas of India at the time of the Raj. Nair traditions still gave the women a status and a freedom they enjoyed nowhere else in the subcontinent. Christian traditions laid a great stress on education. The people of Cochin and

Travancore were then – as they still are – the most literate of Indians, even if, in terms of high culture, they may have to defer to the Brahmins of Madras. And the rulers of these states, who for reasons of protocol were accorded the northern Indian title of maharajah, were among the small group of native princes who actively prepared their people to participate in government decades before British rule came to an end.

Driving from Cochin to Trivandrum, once the capital of Travancore and now of the modern state of Kerala, Inge and I were travelling familiar country, the borderland between these two ancient states, which more than any other area is the heartland of Kerala. Much had changed. After we left the outskirts of Cochin, passing the baroque Portuguese churches that lingered beside marshes white with feeding egrets, we travelled for long stretches on a broad new highway – unusually well made for India – instead of on the narrow seacoast roads of our earlier visits to the Malabar Coast where the palm fronds almost met overhead. Some of the canals that had once been crowded with country craft were now brilliant with the lilac-coloured flowers of the clogging water hyacinth. In Allepey, the first town down the road, many of the old factories where workers had once woven coconut matting on immense wooden handlooms were deserted and falling into decay.

There were changes, too, in the way people lived and the way life treated them. When we first came to Kerala, elephantiasis was a common sickness; one saw many sufferers with grotesquely swollen limbs, and men with gigantically swollen testicles; now, on this whole day's journey, I saw only one man with a mild case of "Cochin leg," as it used to be called, and he was elderly. I saw also only one old woman with uncovered, wrinkled breasts, whereas seventeen years before, the custom of women going bare-topped, which the local Brahmins had imposed on the lower castes, was still common.

Not only did it seem that regressive customs were vanishing, there were also signs of greater prosperity. Here and there we would pass, prominent in the midst of a rice paddy, a new white-stuccoed villa with bright painted doors and windowframes of a kind never seen in the old Kerala, where most people were very poor and where the rich dressed modestly in white shirt and *lungi* (waistcloth) like the rest and, if they had large houses, sheltered them well behind trees. Simplicity of appearance was an almost religious virtue among the traditional Malayalis, and even their characteristic temples tend to be modest wooden structures in comparison with the elaborate stone structures of the Tamils with their massive *gopurams* or gate-towers.

In Quilon, an old town halfway on our journey that had slept a long sleep since the last Chinese junks left in the sixteenth century, there was a rash of new stores selling appliances, a Honda car agency (though we had seen no Hondas on the road), and a big garish hotel built by Iranian refugees, and so empty that three waiters served four of us with our coffee and Britannia biscuits.

A tall Sikh was the only other guest: a building contractor who had come down to share in this unexpected boom in what had once been one of the poorest corners of India. He joined us for the pleasure of seeing fellow strangers in a region that in language and traditions was as foreign to him as it was to us.

"You're right," he said. "It's all oil money. The chaps you see building what they think are pukka houses which everyone will envy are the Johnny-come-latelies of the boom. Chaps who went to Kuwait and made good on a failed Matric. When the bottom falls out of oil, it's going to end, and not with a bang but a whimper." He looked at me with a sly expectancy. "Old Possum, what? Took my degree in English and haven't read a book since. Mark my words, one of these days the mobs will be out burning those bright new houses, and burning this hotel as well. They burnt shops in Trivandrum yesterday. Look out for the police down there. They get nervous in riots, and then they shoot. Much more dangerous than the mob!"

But beside this new Kerala of unexpected prosperity and conspicuous spending and communal unrest, the old one continued, in many ways unchanged; after all, only a minority could possibly benefit from the windfall profits of the Persian Gulf. Most of the people still worked hard in traditional ways for little profit. In the coconut groves, the women span coir cord on enormous wheels at the end of long rope runs. Man was still, as in the old Kerala, the most visible beast of burden. In the whole journey from Ernakulum to Trivandrum – well over two thousand kilometres – we saw only two bullock carts. The place of animal-drawn vehicles was taken by big carts rigged for two men to drag and often transporting immense burdens. Even bicycles had been adapted for freight, and men with straining calves transported such large cargoes on these specially built carriers that we were amazed they managed to sustain enough momentum to keep their balance. Yet they never faltered. And they rarely rebelled, except by occasionally voting communist, though communist governments had done little to lower the wall between rich and poor, which still seems as high and solid as anywhere else in India.

From the beginning we were sceptical about our driver, Thomas, a smaller and even blacker man, who our taxi-driver in Ernakulum told us was his brother and completely reliable. We soon realized he knew little about the roads outside Cochin, and at Quilon, instead of taking the coast road directly to Trivandrum, he drove on to a side route that led eastward toward the Western Ghats and the jungles on the boundary of Tamilnad. Whether he acted from ignorance or calculation we were never sure, but we had difficulty inducing him to turn off on a road farther inland that would take us to Trivandrum, even then by a sinuous hilly way that would prolong our day's travel by a couple of hours, and notably increase the mileage we would have to pay for. We decided to dismiss him in Trivandrum and find local drivers who knew the terrain.

Still, it was a pleasant region he had misled us to, a land of small hills that would sometimes surge out of the green, abundant vegetation in bold whalebacks of grey rock. Except for the bare surfaces and the small pockets of scrub to the windward of them, the whole countryside was cultivated, and everything in nature seemed to be put to use, for even the trees that might not yield a commercial crop provided necessary shade for those that did. It was the region of Kerala that in the two millennia from the coming of early Greek mariners to the arrival of the East India Company provided the spices – and especially the pepper for which, as Pliny once complained, the Roman Empire was being drained of gold – that made the Malabar coast such a desirable terrain for imperialists.

Tiled wooden houses hid in the groins between the hills, and there were villages centred on typical Keralan temples, which are built of wood – a kind of stockade to keep out the unfaithful – with elaborately carved gateways resembling those of Nepali temples, each with a sanctuary inside that has a great conical roof supported on low walls.

The crops in this rich land were of extraordinary variety. Every level piece of ground was a jade green lake of rice paddy, and in the palm groves retreating up the hillsides, the coconuts were varied by the slender green trunks of areca palms (whose nuts are eaten with betel leaf) and the stubby boles of oil palms. Whole slopes were covered in groves of cashews or mangoes, in plantations of tapioca or coffee, the latter shaded by red-flowered flame trees, while shuttlecock papaya trees and green-bannered banana plants were close to the houses for daily gathering. Dark cascades of pepper vines spilt like ivy wherever there were dead or dying trees to support them. Outside the houses the people laid out their produce to dry in the sun; sometimes it was brown rice, sometimes copra chips, but most often in this region it was peppercorns, green at first but darkening into black before they were finally gathered up. This was a far more abundant land than the more crowded coast, and the substantial-looking farmhouses, sometimes double-roofed, with the broad verandas characteristic of inland Kerala, suggested a tradition of prosperity.

By the winding roads of this green foothill country, we rode down into Trivandrum, a city built, like Rome, on seven hills. Here the flat littoral of Malabar gives way to rocky coasts as the land begins to narrow to the tip of India and the Ghats come close to the sea.

15. City of the Serpent

We did not stay in the city at Trivandrum but drove on through the low tangle of coastal hills to Kovalam. Inge and I had known Kovalam in the past as a place of poor fishing villages, but now a large hotel spilled in a concrete cascade down the cliff of a high headland toward the long, sickle bay with its wide golden strands. Kovalam Beach was built by the Indian government to attract tourists, and it shared most of the faults of state-run establishments; dead spiders filled the corners of the ill-swept rooms and the French-titled meals in the restaurant were among the least edible we encountered in India. We went there in mutual resignation; none of us was interested in the kind of organized idleness to which such places are devoted, but we were tired after our weeks of travel and needed a pause. And Kovalam Beach had some compensations, partly because of the panoramic vastness of its setting, and partly because the local fishing people who regarded the beaches as their own terrain had encapsulated it in their lives as an oyster encapsulates a foreign substance.

Predictably, whether they were Indian or foreign, the visitors stayed mostly on the private beach at the base of the cliff, where the Europeans stripped down and toasted themselves browner than any Indian would wish to be; the Indians kept their clothes on and took timid trips in the fishy-smelling catamarans, consisting of five coconut logs bound by coir rope, which the local boys hired out when they were not riding them through the surf for close inshore fishing. The serious fishing was done by net, and it was a memorable sight, viewed from the clifftop.

The long net was attached to a rope held by a team on shore, while a large high-prowed boat of sewn planks that looked like a Viking long-ship took the net in a wide semicircle until it finally returned to shore. There it was beached and the crew leapt out and seized their own rope, and the two teams together hauled in the net while other fishermen circled around and loudly beat the sides of smaller dugouts with their paddles to drive the fish to shore ahead of the net.

The local people had no intention of ceding the great beach to strangers. They had their own shrines there: a small white Hindu temple with a red flag, from which at odd hours we would hear the hoarse blaring of the conch, and, set in a little amphitheatre of rocks, a mosque with a green flag, from which every two hours the voice of the muezzin would float faintly up to us. The country women bathed there, wading fully clothed into the surf and emerging with their saris provocatively moulded against their bodies. I would wander on this beach while Toni was catching sunburn as he sat painting the aquamarine Arabian Sea breaking over the grey rocks of the headland, and always I would be waylaid: by a man with a green coconut in one hand and a machete poised to scalp it for my benefit in the other; by a boy who would emerge out of a cluster of rocks where smoke was rising to ask always, "What is your name?", and then invite me to an *al fresco* fish fry; and once by an urgent young man who shouted, "You want a boat, master? I take you out for thousand rupees!" "What a joke!" I answered, and suddenly we broke together into laughter, united by the preposterousness of the thought, and I gave him ten rupees and went peacefully on my way.

The best time at Kovalam was the half hour before dusk when the western sea shone like a god's shield of shimmering electrum before the sun fell with tropical speed below the horizon. We would wander then, as the air cooled with the incoming breeze, searching out the small, delicate flowers in the rock clefts, often as vivid as the tiny blossoms of the Arctic, and watching the splendid soaring of the kites on the evening wind, and especially the Brahminy kites which were common here, splendid birds with white heads and breasts and bright rust-red wings that glowed like burnished enamel in the glancing sunlight.

There were a few minor hotels along the clifftop at Kovalam, patronized by less wealthy Indian holiday-makers, a few fish restaurants, and some stands made of worn driftwood planks that sold gassy drinks and cigarettes and beedies. To renew our dwindling supplies of travellers' necessities and find new places for Toni to paint, we had to go back into Trivandrum. We would drive up the sharply twisting cliff road where twice we missed death by inches when military jeeps came careening round curves on the wrong side of the road, and then we had to traverse an area where the rocks had been cut away on each side of the road and the local fisherwomen and their children sat under ingenious shades made of two or three intertwined coconut branches, involved for a dollar a day or less in what we had now come to recognize as India's most widespread means of solving the problem of rural unemployment: the chipping of stone into road metal.

Trivandrum is a south Indian city, not planned by any alien conqueror, that grew naturally within its seven-hilled landscape into the kind of open urban phenomenon which in more pretentious cultures we would call a garden city and justify with elaborate theories. Victims of a punishing climate, the inhabitants of the Indian subcontinent, whether original Dravidians or later Aryans or invading Muslims, have all sought ways to use space and wind and the breathing of vegetation to comfort them in the hot and humid seasons. And more than most other Indian towns, Trivandrum has remained a traditional southern garden city, in fact if not in name. Its skyline is still low and dominated by good red tile brought from the foothills of the Ghats; the absence of massive buildings means that the sea winds still move freely between its various hills, cooling the air and taking away the fumes of the ever-increasing motor traffic. One end of the city is dominated by the neo-classical colonnades of the old Secretariat of princely pre-independence days, and the other end by the tall *gopuram*, or ceremonial gateway, covered with painted terracotta figures of the deities, of the Sri Padmanabhaswamy Temple where once the maharajahs would impersonate the god. Nobody has been encouraged to build skyscrapers, and in fact the only people to make recent changes to the city were the Muslim rioters who a couple of days ago had burnt a few shops and cafés in the fort area.

In that traditional heart of the city there was indeed an excess of uniforms: paramilitary guards from the Malabar Special Police with vizored helmets and automatic rifles, brought down from Calicut in the northern part of the state, where they were originally recruited by the British in the 1850s to deal with peasant uprisings. The sharp-witted people of Trivandrum observed and then ignored and absorbed them, so that life was going on with a quiet Malayali propriety, as if no torch had been lit and no fire blazed in anger a couple of evenings before. The truth, I suspect, knowing Kerala and its people, was probably that everyone in Trivandrum, whether he threw a brick or kept miles away, was aware and embarrassed that there had been a break in the elaborate protocol of social accommodations by which, for so long there, devout Jews and strict Muslims, pious Christians and caste-oriented Hindus, had managed to live together in such exemplary if uneasy harmony. To quote the Syrian Christian masseur who pounded Toni's muscles at Kovalam: "The Keralans are gentle people, good God-fearing people." I am not sure how that really equates with the traditions of the Nair warrior caste of these parts, yet it was the Nairs who in 1959–60 led with true Gandhian discipline the non-violent campaign of civil disobedience that brought to an end the state's first Communist government. But that is dipping into history that may be unrepeatable, since, like most of India, the Malabar coast has now left the time of ideological politics for an era when caste and community once again determine how a man votes; this means there will probably be a resurgence of insurrection by groups who find they have not great enough numbers to gain their ends in the ordinary democratic way, through elections. In comparison with many other ex-colonial countries, in Asia as much as Africa, India is a remarkable example of the survival of democratic process, but it would be unwise to assume that its contemporary democracy is ruled any longer by Gandhi's belief that a single man inspired by the truth can change the world.

In the still centre of the fort area of Trivandrum, around the great temple, there was little sign of the disturbances that a couple of nights before had put the state capital in the headlines of Indian newspapers. Men were sitting to talk quietly on the steps of the temple tank before going in for their ritual dips and gargles, and washerwomen were adding a grey tinge from its waters to the linen they bashed with button-breaking vigour. In front of the tank ran a narrow street of Brahmin houses painted in red and white vertical stripes, with elaborate yantra patterns auspiciously executed in rice flour before their thresholds.

A broad-hanging peepul tree in this street was sacred to the nagas or serpent gods; around it clustered small upright stones roughly carved like the hooded heads of cobras, and splashed with vermilion powder or garlanded with marigolds. By name Trivandrum is the City of the

Sacred Serpent, which is generally assumed to be Anantha, the giant snake on which Vishnu is said in Hindu legend to have reclined in the dream out of which he created the world. In reality the name probably has older, pre-Hindu origins, for the Nair warrior caste, dominant in Kerala before the arrival of the Aryan Brahmins, derived its name, like the Naga tribesmen of Assam and the Newar caste of Nepal, from an ancient serpent cult that long antedates Hinduism; even today the temples frequented by Nairs in Kerala have little snake groves, with resident serpents, through which we would always tread with due circumspection.

Toni would find his place beside the sacred tank of the Sri Padmanabhan Temple, and sketch with a constant though shifting audience, while the rest of us went off on those shopping expeditions in which, in Indian provincial towns, the search for a single item can lead one through half a dozen murky little general stores where the goods are shown in dirt-filmed glass cases and the salesmen still, with the Indian mania for paperwork, write chits that must be handed to a cashier who slowly enters the transaction in a ledger before releasing one's purchase of three or four rupees. Familiar items like facial tissues were unavailable in Trivandrum, though they are made in India; we even found it impossible to buy vanilla beans, though they are locally grown and used to be plentiful and cheap in Kerala. The only goods readily available were fruit on the outside stalls, "foreign liquors" (which usually meant Indian-made whisky, gin and brandy), and books. As for the latter, the Indian government, stingy in its release of foreign exchange, for some misguided reason allows considerable funds to buy inferior American bestsellers, which are much easier to find in India than the works of the country's own excellent writers with world reputations like R.K. Narayan, Raja Rao, Salman Rushdie and Nirad Chaudhuri, let alone the many Malayali vernacular writers who seldom achieve English translation, though it is the only way they are likely to become known to the general Indian public, with its own fourteen different languages. Shopping in such circumstances could easily consume two or three hours, and in that time, working with the speed of a sure eye, Toni might have completed two fine watercolours and be ready to escape from his observers. Here, the audience was mostly men who came to bathe in the holy waters and then to sit in the sun on the broad steps that surrounded the tank on every side.

16. Land's End of India

Trivandrum is about eighty kilometres from Cape Comorin or Kanyakumari, where the wedge tip of India divides the Arabian Sea from
the Bay of Bengal. Our trip there was a journey of transformations,
for both the landscape and the cultures changed completely in that
comparatively short distance. Kerala ends about fifty kilometres north
of Kanyakumari. Like most Indian states it has boundaries determined
by language, and the people on both coasts at the tip of India are Tamils,
not Malayalis, and are darker, more heavily built, less impeccably tidy.
The domination of the coastal landscape by coconut groves soon comes
to an end, and the land opens into wide rice paddies, water hyacinth
marshes where the buffalo wallow, clear small lakes where big roseate
lotus blossoms stand high in their stalks above the surface of the water.
It is, once again, a country of cattle, with scrawny, reverenced cows
snatching food from around the stalls in the village bazaars and bullocks
taking the place of men between the shafts of carts. Watching the people
at work in their fields, I realized how much Kerala was actually a
horticultural economy, dependent on groves and orchards, on gardens
and small plots growing expensive crops like pepper, the kind of economy in which a large population might survive by intensively using a
small amount of land; this, on the other hand, was an agricultural
economy, extensive in its use of land, expansive in its broad blue un-
shaded skies, so different from those of Kerala, where much of the time
the light was green, filtered through the trees that spread their fronds
like hands across the sky.

Even the shapes of the land seemed to change with the culture. The
nearer we got to Cape Comorin, the narrower grew the corridor of
flat land between the mountains and the coast, and the Western Ghats
crept ever nearer, first as a distant blue lifting of the horizon, and finally
as splendid dolomitic crags, dense jungle hanging in their groins and
humped outcrops of bare, smooth rock – those stony elephant backs
again! – serving as the foothills; here the laterite soil took on a hot red
colour that made the walls of the adobe houses glow in the noonday
sun with a preternatural vividness.

Cape Comorin is one of the great pilgrim centres of India, an oblig-
atory stop for anyone who wishes to make the boast that he has visited
all the most holy sites of Hinduism, an achievement putting one in a
category resembling that of a hajji among Muslims. Even approaching

the cape, we began to sense the sacredness of the area, as, about twenty kilometres from the land's end, the tall gopuram of the great temple of Suchindram, itself a notable place of pilgrimage, towered up over the rice paddies and we drove into the small town and past the sacred tank, with its classically carved water temple and the painted Brahmin houses fringing its banks, to the high walls of the temple, where two carts for carrying the gods in procession, their wheels as tall as a man and their structures covered with elaborately carved wooden panels, rose thirty feet into the air under their shelters of mats.

Tamil Hindus are less fanatical than their Malayali counterparts in keeping infidels out of their temples, and at Suchindram a trio of wiry old men idling under the gopuram were eager to take us inside. Toni stayed outside; his way of painting made interiors less than a priority. But my way of writing makes me curious about interiors of all kinds, and so Yukiko and Inge and I went with the three old men. The women had merely to take off their shoes and stockings; I had to go both barefoot and bare-torsoed, stripping off my shirt and draping around my waist a check lungi, the sarong-like cloth south Indians wear instead of the tucked dhoti of the north. The lungi constricted my walk, and without my shirt I felt a pallid monster in comparison with the lean, licorice-brown old men, their mouths red with betel juice, who were our guides.

We set off along the great outer cloisters – long corridors with dramatic receding perspectives created by lines of richly carved pillars, all in perfect alignment. "All made by man," declared one of the old guides, and then, in an afterthought, "with help of elephant." It struck me then, as it had never done before, that the massive lavishness of the south Indian temples, compared with those of the north, may be due more than anything else to the greater availability of those powerful and intelligent beasts whom nature has given, in their trunks, the nearest things in attached tools to human hands; in structures that required the lifting and careful placing of large pieces of stone, they must have played the role of highly mobile and adaptable cranes.

We walked on, peering into dim shrines where grease-blackened images were barely visible in the light of guttering ghee lamps that burnt behind wire screens before them. All at once we heard the sound of temple music, and a small procession came in sight: a drummer, a man playing a shrill reed instrument that looked like an hautbois, two other men carrying little pendant oil lamps, and two tall, skinny Brahmins holding on their heads, above their painted brows, garlanded and well-polished silver images – one of the Lord Siva and the other of the Lord Vishnu. They went sweeping past us to the sound of music and gruffly chanted mantras. But a little way ahead, there was a sudden confused halt. An unanticipated draught had blown out the flames of the oil lamps, and none of the celebrants carried in his scanty dress the means to relight them. We also stopped, as much out of curiosity as deference. There was a hurried discussion between the temple servants and our guides. The oldest of the guides came up to me, and whispered behind his hand: "Master have matches?" Inge had a box and gave it to him. He stepped forward and laid it on the stone floor of the cloister. One of the lamp-bearers picked it up without looking at us. When the lamps were relit, he laid the matches on the ground and our guide retrieved them. All this time, the two Brahmins had been ostentatiously looking away, not wishing to witness this underhanded commerce with infidels. The drummer beat again, the priests resumed their march, and as they did so, one of them turned his head, caught my eye, and sardonically grinned. A smile of thanks? Of complicity? Of derision? I am still not sure.

Of course, we were not let into the inner sanctuary; even in the most open of Indian temples, that is always kept from the uninitiated. But we saw extraordinary statuary in the lush southern styles, some of it of stone that rang like a sonorous bronze bell when one put one's ear to it and the guide banged with the flat of his hand. Most awesome was a colossus of the monkey god Hanuman, carved out of a single piece of stone eighteen feet high, and garlanded not with flowers but with long chains of leaves, as befitted a sylvan deity.

We had encountered no beggars in Kerala, but at Suchindram they crowded around us when we left the temple: old people and lepers and young women whom we saw pinching their babies to make them cry pitifully; our guides, in turn, set up a great cry of: "We are very poor men!" when we gave them the recognized tip of five rupees each, but went off happily with the addition of a single small note. This was nothing, however, compared with the Lourdes-like atmosphere of Kanyakumari, where the whole long street leading down to the temple on the shore was lined with booths selling votary items and noisy with Indian film music, and the garbage lay thick in the gutters. "Very dirty place!" our driver remarked with a disgusted look; he was a Syrian Christian and as fastidiously clean as most Keralans.

We made our way through the clamour and the ugliness to the temple and the steps beyond it that led down to the beach. A heaving turquoise sea beat into white foam on the rocks, and beyond, a host of catamarans were sailing, their triangular lateen sails up, so that they looked like the fins of a school of gigantic sharks. The land probed out in a scatter of rocks, forming a natural breakwater between the Arabian Sea and the Bay of Bengal and ending in a rocky islet on which a pretentious shrine had been built as a monument to the twentieth-century sage, Vivekananda. Even Vivekananda had become an object of pilgrimage; a big, heavily laden old launch with a sagging canvas awning lurched through the waves from the shore to moor at the rock and discharge its cargo of a couple of hundred passengers.

There was nothing much to do at Kanyakumari unless one were a pilgrim. I wrote up my notes in a quarter of an hour, and then the three of us, Yukiko, Inge and I, looked in the rock pools, which had surprisingly dull fauna compared with those of northern seas, and sought places to read while Toni found himself a rock shelf to paint from and went to work with his usual stoical disregard for the less pleasant aspects of his setting. Eventually, I walked out to join him. The tide was coming in, but there was a stretch of rock that was obviously submerged only in spring tides, and I walked along this; I had to pick my way with care, so thickly were human turds deposited here, at one of the most sacred spots in India. It was somewhat like seeing the close of Canterbury Cathedral turned into a public latrine; and I now understood the driver's disgust. But Toni had found an excellent spot for viewing the Vivekananda Rocks and produced a couple of paintings that satisfied him: the heavy whiff of human ordure seemed to perturb him not at all. As we delicately stepped away, all he said – in a tone of quasi-scientific speculation – was "How strange that such small people produce such enormous droppings!" "It's the vegetarian diet," was all I could answer. "Just think of the elephants!"

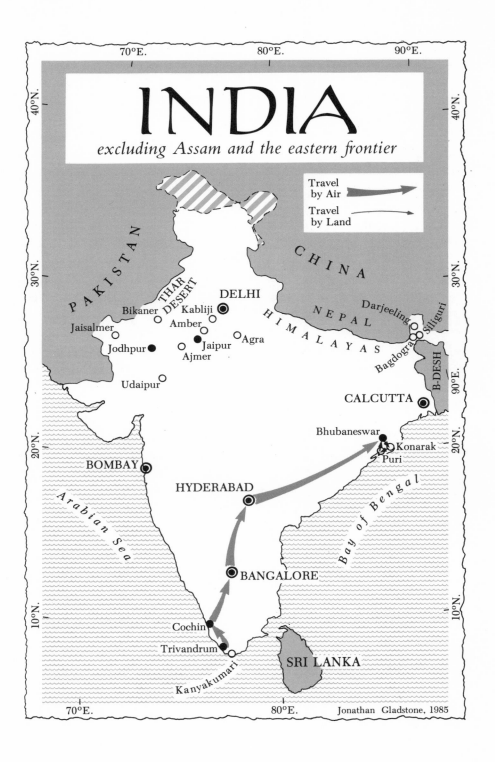

INDIA
excluding Assam and the eastern frontier

Travel by Air
Travel by Land

PAKISTAN

CHINA

THAR DESERT

DELHI

NEPAL

Darjeeling
Siliguri
Bagdogra
B-DESH

HIMALAYAS

Bikaner
Kabliji
Amber
Jaisalmer
Agra
Jodhpur
Jaipur
Ajmer

Udaipur

CALCUTTA

BOMBAY

Bhubaneswar
Konarak
Puri

HYDERABAD

Arabian Sea

Bay of Bengal

BANGALORE

Cochin
Trivandrum

SRI LANKA

Kanyakumari

Jonathan Gladstone, 1985

Mukteswara and Siddeswara temples, Bhubaneswar, Orissa

Mnteswara and Siddheswara Temples Bhubaneswar orissa India January 11 1962

The god Nandi, Bhubaneswar, Orissa

The god Nandi, Bhubaneswar, Orissa, India. January 17, 1985

Kanchenjunga Mountain, from Darjeeling

Kanchenjunga Mountain from Darjeeling, January 16 1903

Tibetan chöten, Darjeeling

Tibetan Chörten, Darjeeling, India. January 17, 1965 onley

IV

ORISSA

January 7–13, 1983

17. Echoes from the Raj

From Trivandrum we planned to go to Orissa on the Bay of Bengal, perhaps the best region of India to see ancient temple architecture, since it contains not only thousands of medieval shrines – some abandoned and ruined, but many still the centres of active religious life – but also cave hermitages of Jain and Buddhist monks which date from before the Christian era, and the earliest known monuments connected with the great Indian king, Ashoka. We made the journey in three hops across central India, stopping for a couple of days in Bangalore and a single night in Hyderabad.

Flying north from Trivandrum, we passed over the great green sea of palm groves until we began to descend toward the immense mirrors of shallow water that surround Cochin. From Cochin we flew inland, northeastward over the dark carpets of tea plantations in the high valleys of the Ghats and the jungle-pelted ridges where megalithic men built stone circles remarkably like those of Britanny and Cornwall. The Deccan, the vast arid central plateau of India, passed below us, great horseshoes of austere hills clasping areas of cultivation within their curves, until we reached Bangalore, grown, since last we saw it a decade before, into a small metropolis whose suburban housing settlements spread far into the surrounding hills. Bill Davinson, a former Indian Army officer and head of the Mysore Resettlement and Development Agency (Myrada), with whom Inge and I had worked for many years resettling Tibetan refugees in southern India, was there to meet us, with his assistant, Aloysius Fernandez, a young Indian Catholic who had left the priesthood to devote himself to the rehabilitation of Indian rural life.

Bangalore was built by the British as an administrative capital when they governed the native state of Mysore from 1831 to 1861, after which they returned the region to princely rule, and now it is the capital of the state of Karnataka, which was constituted after independence. It has perhaps retained more of the good qualities of the cities of the Raj than any other place in India. Its winter climate is dry and rather cool, its centre is open and airy: wide streets, parks and racecourses separate the shopping areas, fountains abound, and enormous old trees planted in the early Victorian era and carefully preserved; even a statue of the King Emperor Edward VII stands undisturbed among the bright flower beds of a public garden.

The West End Hotel, where we stayed, keeps up the spirit of a good imperial hostelry more faithfully than any other Indian hotel I know, with its long verandas and shady lawns, and the local people pay surprising deference to it. At every table occupied by Indian businessmen and bureaucrats, only one language was being spoken: English. They reminded me of the Russian aristocrats in tsarist days who spoke only French. In other facilities for a civilized life Bangalore is equally well provided; Prince's Restaurant and Higginbottom's bookshop are as good as anything of their kind in India. There is also a splendid antique emporium. When we entered it and the proprietor, a small compact man, came up to us, we recognized him as an old acquaintance. Eighteen years before, when we were gathering material for my book on Kerala, Mr Natesan – we never knew his first name – kept a little store in a Trivandrum bazaar. We bought a wood carving that had been part of a temple cart from him then, and a few small bronzes, and admired another wood carving we felt we could not afford; Christmas Day came two days later, and a messenger arrived with a brown paper parcel; it contained the carving we had admired, a gift from Natesan. We had always remembered that act of typically Keralan generosity, and so we were glad to see him again, prospering after so many years, and to buy a fine wood carving from Tanjore of the god Vishnu out of his back room.

The Karnatakans themselves have something of the natural grace and comeliness of behaviour that had pleased us among the Malayalis in Kerala. We arrived at an especially eventful time in Indian political history, for Mrs Gandhi's Congress (I) party had just deservedly been defeated in the January 1983 elections, after a shameless record of corruption and nepotism in local affairs, in the two great southern states of Karnataka and neighbouring Andhra Pradesh. In Andhra Pradesh, there had been no doubt of the landslide victory of the film star Rama Rao and his Telugu regionalist party, but in Karnataka no single party had emerged with clear victory, and the governor of the state had refused to transfer power until the opposition groups could convince him they had formed an alliance that would not fall apart, as such arrangements tend to do in India, within months of the coalition taking office. During the day of indecision, a huge crowd waited outside the governor's mansion, watched over by city policemen in blue helmets like London bobbies (Bangalore also has red double-decker buses) and by state police in khaki uniforms with slouch hats pinned up at the sides like those of Australian soldiers. But there was no noise and turbulence as there might have been in Delhi, and certainly would have been in Calcutta, at such a time. The crowd waited silently, convinced, to all appearance, that justice would be done.

Toni and Yukiko spent their time in Bangalore up in the Nandi Hills, where Toni painted the sombre old temples dedicated to the worship of the bull god Nandi, companion of Siva, while Inge and I talked to Davinson and Fernandez about the possibility of extending Canada India Village Aid's help to South India. We were anxious to vary our aid by applying it to schemes more basic than Patwant Singh's rather sophisticated hospital at Kabliji, and they were seeking an organization that would join Myrada in a scheme for helping the Gond tribespeople who lived on the borders of Andhra Pradesh and Orissa in a forested region of South India. Apart from rather primitive rice cultivation, the Gonds lived by gathering forest products: wild medicinal plants; the cocoons of the tussore moth which yield a fine silk; rosewood. But for generations they had been exploited by Hindu traders because they had no numbers higher than twenty, the sum of fingers, thumbs and toes, and they would often accept twenty rupees for an item worth many times as much in the market. Myrada had no intention of changing the Gonds' way of life, except by helping them upgrade their rice cultivation and form a selling cooperative to prevent their being exploited by the traders. They also wanted to send in some paramedics to set up a little dispensary and teach basic health rules. It was this they asked us to fund, and we took back the request to our board in Canada. It became CIVA's second Indian project.

On the day we left, we saw nothing of the land between Bangalore and Hyderabad, for once again the Indian Airlines planes were running hours late, and the sun set in orange splendour as we waited at Bangalore airport. We had missed Hyderabad on our previous visits to India but what we saw of it in the darkness, and early the following morning, was in no way tempting. The buildings of the Nizam's day were largely crumbling away, and the roads were impeded by construction projects that appeared to have been abandoned halfway to completion. The hotel where we stayed was new, dirty, expensive, and crowded with politicians; Hyderabad is the capital of Andhra Pradesh, and the place-seekers were gathering like vultures to feast under the new dispensation of Rama Rao, just elected to power. If the decrepit look of the city could be taken as a manifestation of the effects of government by Mrs Gandhi's Congress party, it had obviously been high time for a change.

18. A Grove of Perfect Beings

Bhubaneswar, on the other hand, immediately attracted us, and continued to do so. It lies down over the hills that border the Deccan – this time the Eastern Ghats – in the green alluvial plain beside the Bay of Bengal. Until India became independent, Bhubaneswar was mainly a religious centre, and the core of its old town still clusters around the great Lingaraja – or Kingly Penis – Temple, one of the holiest shrines in all India, dedicated to the Lord Siva in his phallic manifestation. But in 1948, Bhubaneswar replaced Cuttack, the old British provincial capital, as the administrative centre of Orissa, and a new-built quarter came into being, of low, modern structures in gardens bright with a bewildering variety of tropical flowers. (One of the miracles of India is that, with so many people, there always seems to be enough room – working with instinct as much as deliberation – to create towns that are well spaced and do not run upward to shut out the sun.)

We stayed in the new town at a government hotel that, surprisingly, was well run and friendly too. Until recently, despite its extraordinary relics, Orissa has lain off the main Indian tourist routes, and the Oriyas receive strangers with much spontaneous good will. It was to the old city that we constantly gravitated, for here, in a profusion rivalled in my experience only in the great Buddhist centre of Pagan in Burma, we found the relics of a golden age of devotion and creation that had lasted almost a millennium, from the Hindu revival that displaced a dominant Buddhism in the seventh century A.D., down to the Mogul conquest of Orissa in the sixteenth century.

Once there must have been a vast city here – one of those typical South Asian cities like Angkor Thom in Cambodia where, in the early centuries, the buildings in which men, including even kings, lived and worked were made of perishable materials, wood and bamboo, and stone was reserved for the sacred edifices. In the tempests of history the houses and even the palaces vanished, and the temples remained.

Around the Lingaraja, where pilgrims have been numerous for nearly a thousand years, such a continuity has indeed resulted in a closely inhabited quarter of narrow streets with big hostels or *dharamsalas* in which wandering devotees can stay. The old houses of this quarter are built of rust-red pumice stone and often thatched with reeds, but some of them have extraordinary façades of coloured cast iron, delineating ancient myths with a brilliant naiveté that resembles the folk art – the gaudy pottery and papier-mâché figures – to be found everywhere in Orissa, on wayside stalls as well as in the stuffy handicrafts emporia which the state government operates. Religion in India, as in medieval Europe, never really dissociated itself from commerce; the money-changers, by some door or another, always managed to appear at the temple. And when we circled the Lingaraja, passing the Lion Gate and the Elephant Gate and the Tiger Gate and the Horse Gate, each with its freshly painted animal guardians, there were always, facing the high walls of the temple compound, and clustering under them, the stalls and shops of which a few sold religious items, but most carried the kind of things one could buy in any bazaar, from fruit and rice and spices to brilliant machine-made cloths and gaudy plastic ware, which in India, as in France, is usually of excellent quality, made for long use rather than quick discarding. One of the stalls, however, had the chunky little animal figures made out of bell-metal by nomadic braziers in the Orissa villages, and we all bought some of them; sturdy caparisoned horses and elephants with gods riding on their backs, as solidly satisfying and heavy in the hand as early Inuit stone carvings.

In Orissa there was no Tamil laxness regarding entry into temples. So far as the large pilgrimage temples were concerned, we were back to Kerala standards of walling out; no infidel could be admitted. But at the Lingaraja no less a figure than Lord Curzon had shown some concern for frustrated European visitors, and had ordered the building of a platform from which they could look into the courtyard of the great shrine, if not into the heart of its sanctuary. We climbed up there with a small boy called Krishnarama who spoke English. Krishnarama pointed out the various buildings that culminated in the *deul* or sanctuary with its immense tower rising above the chamber that housed the image of Siva, which was the main object of worship: the *bhogamandapa* or hall of offering led into the *nata-mandir* or dancing hall, where the *devadasis* or sacred dancer-prostitutes had in a less puritan era enacted the legends of Siva and Parvati, which led in its turn to the *jagamohan* or entrance porch that with the *deul* forms the basic core of all Orissa temples. We saw the structure, indeed, but very little else. We could hear, over a public address system, the ringing of bells and chanting of mantras, so that we assumed a ceremony to the great lingam which represents Siva was going on. We saw people – mostly women – hurrying into the hall of offerings with bamboo trays laden with fruit. And we watched a young long-haired *sanyasin* in an orange dhoti who had seated himself on the flagstones of the courtyard and carried on a puja of his own, with flowers, rice and coconuts, brass vessels and other unidentifiable objects. It was the only worship we were allowed to see in Orissa, though it is one of the great heartlands of Indian piety. Still, we were impressed when Krishnarama, having been so helpful, observed the spirit of Lord Curzon's gift by refusing any kind of payment, particularly as we had no sooner descended than we were surrounded by other boys asking us for pens and "country coins," by which they meant the coins of our own country.

In spite of its daunting exclusiveness, we liked the Lingaraja and its surroundings and Toni came back more than once to look at its splendid and intricately carved tower, perhaps the most beautiful in all India, while the rest of us wandered around its Ocean Drop tank which is said to contain in its murky depths water from every sacred river in India. The Ocean Drop has not only a fine water pavilion where the god is taken from his sanctuary for a bath each year, but also many small shrines around its perimeter. In one spot stood a group of eight such shrines, each consisting of a miniature tower perhaps twenty feet high and an entrance porch tall enough for a short man to stoop into; all of them were covered with carvings depicting sacred legends, and in some of the sanctuaries, when we peered in, we could see ashes and smell the scent of flowers deposited there. An image of Nandi the sacred bull stood among the shrines, its head blackened by the hands that had touched it over the centuries, among them those of a covey of young women who swept past us to dip in the tiny separate tank that belonged to this precinct, and to emerge, wet garments skin-tight over nubile young bodies, and run giggling away.

But what made Bhubaneswar like no other Indian sacred centre I had seen was not the great Lingaraja temple, but the scores of small temples scattered in the fields and lanes where the present town shredded away into its rural outskirts. Most of these temples were built a millennium or more ago, between the seventh and eleventh centuries, when Orissa was ruled by the Kesari dynasty, devout worshippers of Siva. Legend says there were originally seven thousand of them, and that

most were destroyed by fanatical Muslims when the Hindu dynasties
came to an end in the sixteenth century. The remains of at least five
hundred survive, beside the rustic lanes and often hidden in fields and
gardens. One afternoon when Toni was painting a shrine by the roadside, a boy asked him, "Would you like to see my family's temple?"
and took him into a courtyard where he was welcomed by an old farmer
and his wife and taken to a fine little shrine, obviously well cared for
over the centuries, lush with carving and faced by its own little Nandi
figure. The whole family stood around Toni as he painted it and through
the boy, who alone spoke English, they asked the ritual Indian questions
put to strangers: "Where do you come from?" "How many children?"
But they asked no questions about his painting or why he did it, nor,
as far as I can remember, did any other members of his outdoor au-
diences, and this, I suspect, must be due to a rooted feeling, bred of
the notions of karma and caste, that each man has his own destined
calling, which is in a way his mystery.

The small temples around Bhubaneswar would each consist of a
sanctuary, with a tower between thirty and forty feet high and a porch
fifteen or twenty feet high, within a paved and sometimes walled enclosure. There were no plain surfaces; every inch of the outer walls of
sanctuary and porch was covered with intricate carvings of virtually
anything that could be regarded as celebrating the fullness of life, from
lovers caressing and coupling to processions of elephants and horses,
from birds and animals and flowers to the extraordinary series of naga
queens, with their cobra cowls and long serpentine tails, that decorated
the Raj Rani temple. The towers were not pointed like Gothic spires,
but stubby topped, their corbelled shoulders supporting big capstones
rather like the tops of gigantic mushrooms. The mood of the carving
varied, perhaps according to period, from an austere baroque kind of
grandeur to, in some of the smaller shrines, rococo fantasies of miniature
figures.

A few of Bhubaneswar's more neglected temples were greatly eroded,
and tufted with vegetation like picturesque Piranesi ruins, and one at
least had been gripped as if by an octopus in the roots of a young peepul
tree that were prising its stones apart. But some of the oldest temples
were in extraordinary preservation, their carvings almost as crisp and
clear as when the sculptor laid down his chisel.

The best of them were in a small cluster of about twenty temples
called The Grove of Perfect Beings, where they stood like strange stone
fungi among the ancient peepul trees that mostly overshadowed them.

The most exquisitely carved of them all, the Parsurameswar Temple, is said to be the oldest, built around 650 A.D., yet its carvings were astonishingly sharp-edged, and the many animal figures were vigorous and alive. "Every stone has its antic value" my local guidebook remarked, and its unconscious ambiguity was strangely expressive of the gaiety of feeling this ancient shrine projected.

In recent years, many young Brahmins have attached themselves to the smaller temples around Bhubaneswar, perhaps because the older priests have established an irremovable control over the larger temples. Usually these self-appointed guardians of the shrines have had an education beyond mere Hindu dogma and mythology, like the bespectacled man in his yellow *sanyasin's* robe who approached us at Parsurameswar and was unusually fluent in English. He flourished a donation book showing substantial gifts from foreign donors and asked me for ten rupees. I offered two, which he accepted with good grace and lit a candle so that he could take us, respectfully barefooted, into the sanctuary. It contained nothing but the most simple and expressive symbol of the union of the god and his *shakti* – the combined lingam and yoni carved from a single stone, the tip of the lingam crowned with betel leaves and the shaft hung with jasmine garlands. Bats rustled and chirped in the heavy cone of darkness above our heads, and the floor was spattered with their droppings, from which a sharp smell impregnated the air. Standing there, I wondered what in the past had gone on in so many such small temples, and it struck me that the young Brahmins we encountered here and there were probably re-enacting an original pattern, that of hermit priests, each tending his little shrine and receiving a few devotees who brought to altars as simple as we had seen the same kind of gentle offerings. I felt a little mean in my own offering and gave the priest another five rupees, and then we went off to the tank down the road to wash the bat dung off our feet.

19. The Black and the White Pagodas

There are three major temples in Orissa, and they form an isosceles triangle, with the apex at the Lingaraja and the base points on the coast at the Sun Temple in Konarak and the temple of Jagganath in Puri, each place being roughly sixty kilometres from Bhubaneswar. Both of these temples are considerably later than the small shrines at Bhubaneswar, having been built in their present form in the twelfth or thirteenth century by kings of the Ganga dynasty who, unlike their Shaivite Kaseri predecessors, were devotees of the other great Hindu cult god, Vishnu. The temple at Puri is dedicated to Jagganath, lord of the universe, a locally worshipped avatar of Vishnu; that at Konarak is dedicated to Surya, the ancient Vedic sun god.

The great shrine at Puri is unusual in India, since even before Gandhi's campaigns to open the sacred precincts to untouchables, it was open without distinction to all castes and even to those of no caste; every Hindu was welcomed into the presence of the strange images, carved with primitive abstraction out of tree trunks and obviously the relics of some powerful tribal cult incorporated into Hinduism, that represent Jagganath, his brother Balabhadra and his sister Subhadra, who are all worshipped together. Such accessibility is not extended to non-Hindus, however, and since we knew we would be allowed at most to peep from some high place into the temple courtyard, we went there on the same day that we visited Konarak, which is only thirty kilometres away along the seacoast road that forms the base of the isosceles triangle. Both temples are visible out to sea, and in the days of sailing ships, they served as landmarks to mariners bound for Calcutta; the temple of Jagganath, which is always cleanly limewashed, they called the White Pagoda, and the ruined and deserted Temple of the Sun was the Black Pagoda.

The Orissa countryside through which we drove down to Konarak by a little-travelled road had the look of pastoral peace and plenty, the land much less thickly populated than in Kerala. Most of it was rice paddy, in which the men worked with ox ploughs and backhoes, wearing loincloths and roughly twisted turbans and looking remarkably like the figures of peasants we had seen in the Bhubaneswar sculptures. Some of them were irrigating the fields with a curious scoop attached to ropes, which they would dip into a pond or stream and then heave and tip so that it emptied backward into the irrigation channels. Market gardens growing potatoes, cauliflowers and other vegetables had been planted around the villages, probably for the Calcutta market which is only a night away by train, and here scarecrows had been erected, with demoniac faces painted on their calico heads. Every now and then we would pass a high, tightly woven cane fence surrounding a rectangular plot; these were the gardens where the betel vines grew, a valuable crop that needed protection from thieves.

The villages were tiny places of thatched mud or pumice-stone houses, with bright yellow stacks of rice straw standing among them, shaped almost exactly like the little temple towers, even to the extent of having a kind of woven thatch roof like the capstones of the spires. Which had come first, haystack or temple? We noticed, too, that the Oriya villagers, whose methods of cultivation seemed much the same as they had been in the days of the Moguls – perhaps even in Ashoka's days – were not averse to making use of modern phenomena when it suited their purpose. They would strew rice ears across the road so that passing cars squeezed out the grain and saved the threshing; they spread coconut husks in the same manner – an easier way to crush out the fibres than the Keralan method of beating with clubs.

Every village had its large tank surrounded by greenery, the murky water shining blue under the sunlight and bearing on its surface red lotuses and drifts of white flowers that looked like water crowfoot. We were out early and the villagers were performing their ablutions; in one tank I saw a man enthusiastically gargling water he had lifted in his hands, and no more than four feet away, another man squatting down and vigorously scrubbing his behind in the same water. We wondered at a version of "cleanliness next to godliness" that made a fetish of washing the body but took no notice of the filthy water in which it was washed. Was there a metaphor here, I speculated, for India's present political condition where corruption is ignored so long as the patriotic forms continue to be observed?

At Pipli the road divided and we turned right for Konarak. Pipli was a place of mud houses and weatherbeaten plank booths, most of them selling bright appliqué panels – rather like the *molas* (panels of cut and overlaid cloth) made by the Kuna Indians of San Blas in Panama. The village is celebrated in Orissa for this work, the best of which is used as hangings in the temple sanctuaries. Local artistic traditions also found expression in the intricate white patterns, like chalk filigree, with which the walls of the houses were decorated. Our driver told us they honoured the full moon festival for unmarried young men and women that was about to take place.

As we drew nearer to Konarak, the villages became fewer and the land less cultivated. Large marshes harboured flocks of egrets and many paddy birds and fishing cormorants, and from the trees hung the pendulous nests of weaver birds. Then the sand dunes began, piling inland several miles from the coast, and it was here that we came to Konarak's Black Pagoda – not on a sea beach as I had imagined, but among the sandhills from whose grip it had been released early in this century by the archaeologists.

The temple at Konarak was an extraordinary, original and unimitated concept in Indian religious architecture. The sun god Surya, like the Greek sun god Helios, is said to travel in his chariot on the daily journey across the heavens from sunrise to sunset. The great shrine dedicated to him was to be a grand architectural, sculptural representation of his chariot which would at the same time embrace the essential elements of an Orissan temple – towered sanctuary, entrance porch and dancing hall. Twenty-four enormous stone wheels were lined along each side of the base of the structure; seven immense stone horses strained as they hauled the mighty vehicle of which, as in every other local temple, no surface was left uncarved.

Records of Konarak are extraordinarily scanty. We do not know for certain what king built it. We do not even know for sure whether the tower was completed; experts wonder whether the sandy soil could even have borne its weight, though the massive foundations have shown no sign of sinking; it was wind-borne sand that submerged them. Certainly the chronicles of the Mogul period suggest that it was in fact built, for Akbar's historian Abu'l Fadl talks of a building 150 cubits high – about 250 feet – and this can only have been the sanctuary tower.

Desecrated by Muslims, the temple appears to have been deserted by the early seventeenth century. Sand began to drift in, covering the wheels and the straining horses, and the massive capstone seems to have collapsed, removing the key that held the corbelled walls in place. By 1825, according to a British traveller, only a corner of the tower was left standing, "which viewed from a distance gives the ruin a singular appearance, something resembling that of a ship under sail." During a strong gale in 1848, even this remaining fragment fell, and when Rajendrala visited the site in 1868, no more was left of the great tower than "an enormous mass of stones studded with a few pipal trees here and there." The lower buildings were largely protected by the encroaching sand until, in the early twentieth century, the Archaeological Survey – one of the finest services of the British Raj – undertook the uncovering of the great chariot and the shoring up of what remained of the sanctuary tower, so that one can again climb up to the first platform and see the three majestic chlorite figures of Surya, facing with their ineffably serene smiles the sun at its rising, its zenith and its setting.

Grand as the concept of the great temple-chariot originally was, and splendid as it must have appeared when the sanctuary stood to its full height of 260-odd feet, the effect was almost completely destroyed by the tower's collapse, which left a building quite out of classic proportion, with a stump of a tower surviving beside its porch and dancing hall. It was in detail that the Sun Temple remained fascinating, and as I wandered around it I recognized that this was how I had always seen it in illustrations and hence assumed the whole so inevitably magnificent that it must be seen. The spirit of the original concept had abandoned the broken and marred structure as such, but it remained in the component parts: the intricately decorated wheels with lively vignettes of human activities on every spoke; the horse and elephant and lion figures so massive and stone-solid and yet so full of life; the serenely beautiful female musicians in the high galleries of the porch, and the celebrated erotic groups which, irreverently perhaps, I saw as representations less of the ecstasy of sex than of the comedy of man's preoccupation with it, for many of them are certainly best seen as small masterpieces of Rabelaisian fun. There is much in Tantrism – like much in Zen – that, considered less seriously than most western scholars take it, can be interpreted as wise men's laughter at the human condition.

There were no pilgrims at Konarak, and the only hint of religion was a long-haired young man in yellow robe who came with a sweet, disarming smile and hibiscus blossoms in his hand; he told us a few things we already knew, demanded the customary ten rupees, and accepted two; this time my conscience was not in operation. But even without pilgrims, the temple precinct was crowded with visitors, and apart from a small contingent of Japanese and four or five Europeans, they were all Indians, again reinforcing our impression that the people of the country are at last beginning to gain the kind of historical sense which found no place in traditional Hinduism. They spread around in families, photographing each other in front of the images of Surya, chaffering with the pedlars who were selling postcards and fresh coconuts and necklaces of red coral from the beach, and looking at the erotic carvings with the giggling embarrassment that betokens the puritanism of most modern Indians.

There was not a touch of religious devotion in their response; they showed as little emotion as American tourists tramping around Westminster Abbey, and watching them, I wondered what this great temple could have been like in the days of its glory, before it was desecrated and deserted and finally ruined. What ceremonies took place there? What festivals? Was it a grandiose dynastic chapel built only for the glory of the kings who identified themselves with the ancient Aryan warriors, worshippers of Surya, a Vedic god already out of fashion by the time the Black Pagoda was built? Or was it, like the other great temples of the region, once a place of pilgrimage?

If there was ever a town, it has not survived, and this perhaps explains the lack of even vague local traditions about the origin of the shrine. But it is even problematical whether a town did exist, for no relics have been found of it, and the possibility remains that the Sun Temple was the vast votary offering of some king cured of an apparently mortal illness, for in one of his roles Surya was a god of healing.

Another possibility came to my mind as we drove away from Konarak on the new coast road to Puri. It ran through another of those virtually uninhabited stretches of country that so firmly negate the image of overcrowded India: mostly sand dunes, covered with casuarina trees and a kind of scrawny local pine, and at times very much like that heath country called the Landes in France's Gascony.

Not far from Konarak we reached a long and beautiful open beach of pale, almost white sand. A group of young wandering Frenchmen had found it and were plunging naked into the surf, but otherwise it was deserted except for a little booth covered with palm leaves where an old man was selling coconuts and some beautiful shells. We bought some of the coconuts, which he opened so neatly that the tops still remained attached like little lids, and stood drinking the sweet, slightly earthy-tasting liquid and watching a fleet of triangular-sailed fishing boats tacking to and fro out to sea, the farthest of them seeming about to fall over the horizon. A few craft were drawn up on the beach, painted with eyes to ward off evil spirits like the boats Van Gogh used to paint at Les Saintes-Maries de la Mer, with women sitting in their shade to repair nets. Off to one side was a little white shore temple, with no houses of any kind near it. According to the old storekeeper, this shrine, too, was dedicated to the sun god, and once a year there was a festival lasting several days to which thousands of people came, living and sleeping on the beach and then departing. Might not this also have happened at Konarak, which in the days of its glory, before the dunes had drifted upward, must have been right on the seashore? And was it not possible that, as the sea receded and the Sun Temple became deserted, this little shore temple actually took its place and inherited its pilgrim festival?

There was virtually no cultivation in the thirty-odd kilometres between Konarak and Puri, and no habitations except for the reed huts of fishermen on the beaches and some rough shacks inhabited by woodcutters from which the smell of burning pine would sometimes drift across the road. We entered Puri from the south, by way of Gundicha

Garh, the tank with its islanded temple to which the images of Jagganath and his brother and sister are brought during the great summer festival, when they are paraded through the city on the vast raths or ceremonial cars from which we derive the word juggernaut.

Our driver, a light-skinned, compact man named Krishnan, who wore an impeccable white cotton suit at all times, drew up to tell us what he called the "history," by which he meant the local legend connected with the annual journey. Each year, by custom, the priests attending Jagganath diagnosed a sickness in the god, and it was then that he was taken to the Gundicha Mandir – the temple in the lake – where for a week he was treated exactly as if he were an ailing human being. Then, on the seventh day, he would be declared cured, and with his companions placed once again on the cars, which four thousand men would pull back, with great rejoicing, to Jagganath's own temple. Jagganath's car, the real juggernaut, stands nearly fifty feet high, is thirty feet square and moves on twenty-four wheels; once devotees would throw themselves into its path to be crushed in a holy death, but in the present faithless age, it is years since this has happened.

The Sri Jagganath Temple, with its two-hundred-foot tower, dominates the skyline of Puri in the same way as the great medieval cathedrals dominate some of the towns of France, but as a living religious corporation its influence over the city's life is even greater, since there are no fewer than seven thousand Brahmins and temple servants engaged in the multitude of minute and varied ceremonial tasks required to serve these extraordinary deities whose bodies are wooden cylinders, whose faces are grotesque masks, and whose truncated arms make them look like the victims of thalidomide poisoning. While approximately twenty thousand people are regularly sustained from the temple's revenues, they represent only part of those who benefit from the shrine and its pilgrims. There are no fewer than 136 *dharamsalas* catering to pilgrims, not counting the South-East Railway Hotel and dozens of small hotels and boarding-houses, while along the processional route of the Baraband or Grand Road, there are stalls selling little painted replicas of the three gods and other relics and souvenirs; as in all Indian religious centres, the beggars swarm, giving devotees an opportunity for acquiring merit, but always heading for foreigners whose affluence is presumed to be greater.

The temple occupies a ten-acre enclosure in the centre of the town, but it is surrounded by a wall twenty feet high, and at the time we arrived, the building from the roof of which one gets the best view was closed. We drove around the temple walls, past the gates guarded once again by lions and horses, tigers and elephants, and finally found a man who would take us up through an old house – a tenement swarming with poor people in squalid rooms who resented the passage of strangers – to the roof where we could look over the temple wall. But the Sri Jagganath also has an inner wall, and consequently we were unable to see the courtyard, as at the Lingaraja Temple, but only to get a better view of the tower and the roofs of the other buildings. After we came down, there was a long wrangle between Krishnan and the owner of the building about the value of the view. The owner wanted twenty rupees but after much shouting in Oriya, he came down by stages to five, which we paid.

Sri Jagganath himself remained doubly protected from the eyes of the unfaithful, but by now we had seen enough replicas of this extraordinary deity to wonder at the enthusiasms which could draw here the estimated million people who come annually for the car festivals. The cult of Vishnu is in many ways the nobler trend in Hinduism, having absorbed much more of Buddhism than the rival cult of Siva; Buddha even has his place as one of the avatars or incarnations of Vishnu. But this great preserver deity, who has been the subject of much elevated metaphysical and ethical speculation, seems very far from the glorified fetishes who preside at Puri, and it would appear to be a far more elemental devotion that responds to these tribal godlings elevated into the Hindu pantheon. There are so many strange conjunctions in Hinduism that even a sympathetic westerner finds it difficult to understand, let alone accept. It has always seemed to me that Tertullian, with his *"Credo quia impossibile,"* would have made a much better Hindu than he did a Christian. I have a papier-mâché model of the high altar at Puri, which I bought from an old woman in the bazaar that day, before me on a bookshelf as I write; I open the little painted doors and see the gaudy miniatures of the gods staring at me with enormous ghostly eyes, and it is Africa and Melanesia, the great reservoirs of primitive tribal cultures, that come to my mind more than India.

We felt no urge to linger in Puri. Apart from the temple, which was freshly whitewashed and painted, it was a decrepit and neglected town, its buildings stained by the monsoons, its narrow streets full of dirty booths where the flies flourished extravagantly, and its seedy, cheap hotels lined along the waterfront, where the surf-swept yellow sand and the blue water of the Bay of Bengal seemed the only clean things in sight; going out on the road back to Bhubaneswar we passed through one of the poorest-looking shack settlements we had seen on this journey in India. The combination of devotion and dirt, cynical

Jilau Khana, Red Fort, Delhi

Jilau Khana, Red Fort, Delhi   India...January 20 1985

Jantar Mantar (Old Observatory), Delhi

Janta Mantar, (old observatory) Delhi, India. January 20 1983

onley

Mosque of Sher Shah, Purana Qila, Delhi

Sher Shah Gate, Purana Qila, Delhi

commercialism and deep poverty, seems to be characteristic of Indian religious centres, and in this, Bhubaneswar was the exception and a place to which we were glad to return through the gentle, vividly green Orissa countryside.

20. Ashoka's Elephant

On the way to Bhubaneswar we had crossed a brown river, sluggish and dry-season shallow. Legend – physically represented by our driver Krishnan – associated it with one of the most dramatic events of Indian history. In the third century B.C. Orissa was the kingdom of Kalinga, against which Ashoka, the king of the great northern realm of Magadha, had marched in his campaign to fulfil his destiny as Chakravartin, the traditional Indian King of the Wheel who, like the Persian King of Kings, claimed the right to rule over all other rulers. In a bitterly fought battle in the eighth year of his reign, somewhere about 260 B.C., Ashoka defeated the king of Kalinga, but his victory turned to dust in his mind when he stood beside this river and saw it jammed with floating corpses whose seeping blood had stained the water red. With this dark epiphany, the Buddhist teaching of which he had heard came home to him with the force of revelation. He was converted to the faith and renounced forever the use of warfare, choosing a new way of conquest by *dharma*, which for him meant the practice of the social and moral virtues of compassion and non-violence and in general caring for the welfare of all living beings, including animals. On the low ridge of hills, out of which the river ran, a great white structure glittered remotely in the sunlight. It was the modern stupa which the Japanese had recently built to commemorate Ashoka's acceptance of Buddhism.

The following day we drove into the wooded Dhauli hills, in search of the relics of Ashoka that survive there to this day. Once, before the British antiquaries got to work in the early nineteenth century, Ashoka was merely a figure of Buddhist legend, but in the 1820s and 1830s James Prinsep, the assay master of the mints at Benares and later Calcutta, not only identified the Bactrian Greek kings of the Punjab by their coins, but also deciphered the rock inscriptions in ancient Prakrit which establish Ashoka as a monarch in history. These inscriptions were the edicts by means of which Ashoka instructed his officials and his subjects in the new order of the *dharma* he sought to establish.

Up at the top of the Dhauli hills we came to the smooth-cut face of rock outcrop into which the first of the edicts had been carved in

Prakrit, an alphabet derived remotely from the Phoenician and therefore directly related to our own. They were very clearly cut, though the thick wire screen protecting them made it difficult to see them distinctly; however, translations in Oriya and English had been painted on boards that stood beside them. The edicts lamented the great killing in Kalinga, exhorted the people to peace, honesty and hard work, warned the king's officials against injustice, abjured hunting and the sacrifice of animals, ordered the digging of wells and the planting of trees by the roadsides for the convenience of travellers, and the growing of medicinal plants, enjoined "great love of righteousness, great self-examination, great circumspection, great effort." Reading them, one felt a mingling of joy that a king so long ago should have framed such an enlightened plan for existence, and sadness that, two thousand years later, his injunctions had been neither bettered nor sustained as a practical way of living, even in his own country. In one way or another, the inhumanity of our practices has persisted as stubbornly as the ideal of a better life has lingered in men's minds, periodically revived by teachers like Gandhi and his noble disciple Vinoba Bhave, but never completely triumphing at the hands either of prince or of prophet.

Still, standing on that fresh, clear morning under the trees with not a person in sight, and reading those fine injunctions from the dawn of history, we could not fail to be moved by the persistence of that longing for a better life which has at least made our world a better place than it would have been without the Ashokas and the Gandhis. The goat-cropped grass in front of the inscription was thickly starred with minute blossoms of such a bright cerulean blue that it offered a kind of benison, so literally did it seem to mirror "heaven in a wildflower."

Beside the inscribed rock was another outcrop, out of which had been carved, at the same time as the edict, one of the oldest stone sculptures in India. It was the foreparts – head, shoulders, forelegs – of an elephant, quite naturalistically carved, so that he seemed to be emerging from the grey rock; I realized with delight that two thousand years ago, a sculptor must have had my own vision of the big rock outcrops so common in India as sleeping elephants, ready to emerge at any moment from the imprisoning stone. This sculptor had caught the vision on its way out and, with fine artistry, had refrained from completing the figure; the sense of the great beast emerging was far more potent.

Long before the kings of the Kesari dynasty began to build their multitude of temples at Bhubaneswar in the seventh century, the area was already a haunt of holy men, and in the second century B.C., a

hundred years or so after Ashoka, Jain monks patronized by a local king called Kharavela created a kind of Thebaid of hundreds of caves and cells honeycombing the two hills known as Khandagiri and Udaigiri which lie not far away from the Ashoka monuments. Nothing was built; everything – according to the early Jain and Buddhist traditions – was cut out of the rock: not only rough-hewn little chambers where the monks lived and meditated, but also the relief carvings of the twenty-four Tirthankaras, or legendary Jain teachers, that were chipped out of the living rock and in style strongly resembled the figures on the Buddhist stupas at Sanchi and Bharhut, which were roughly contemporary; at a distance the long, open galleries cut into the rockfaces were reminiscent of the later and much more famous central Indian caves of Ajanta and Ellora. While Toni and Yukiko painted, Inge and I sat in the caves, looking out at the woodland that climbed up the hill toward them and inhaling the dense fragrance of a mass of wild mangoes in full bloom. Once we had got rid of a persistent guide we were able to absorb the exceptional serenity of the place, which was so intense that we felt our mental feet dipping into the shallows of some vast reservoir of stored-up spirituality.

After a time, we noticed a lot of movement in the trees below us, and when we went down to look, found that it was caused by a large troop of monkeys dominated by a big, grizzled old male, and including a number of females and young of various ages, from the hairless infants that clung all the time to their mothers' fur, to the slightly older children playing incessantly in the branches, leaping from one to the other and staging mock fights. They were completely undisturbed by our presence, and went on playing as if nobody had been there. However, all this changed when I fetched a bag of peanuts from a stall by the roadside. Then they gathered around us, taking the nuts gently from our hands, but leaping up to try and grab the bag whenever they thought my attention could be distracted. Apart from liking the nuts, they seemed to enjoy human company for its own sake, and when the bag was empty, one of them settled down at Inge's feet, silently looking into her face and holding her legs with its small black hands. There seemed such an accord between animal and woman as to indicate that in a small way the spirit of Ashoka's edicts and of the teachings of the Jain monks who followed him had survived among these holy rocks with the monkeys, the descendants of many generations that had been able to live here without fear of predatorial man, since monkeys in India are everywhere sacred. It shifted one's mental barometer just a shade in the direction of hope.

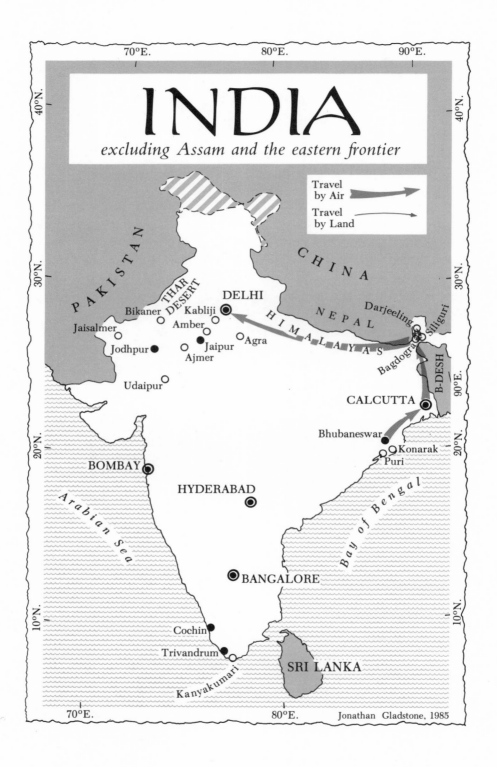

V

DARJEELING

January 13–19, 1983

21. Into the Tall Hills

No corner of India was exempt from the travel difficulties which pla-
gued the country in that cold northern winter, though, since the flight
from Bhubaneswar to Calcutta was a local shuttle, there were no problems for the first day, at least, of our journey to the mountains, and
we reached Calcutta not long after noon. Remembering the taxi drive
into the centre of that appalling city as a particularly daunting one which
we had no desire to carry out twice in a short afternoon, we stayed the
rest of the day at the airport hotel, looking out over the dejected Dum-
dum landscape of palm trees, ponds and decaying British villas, reading,
writing in my journal, eating fish which the Bengalis always cook well,
and carrying on intermittent bargaining, which lasted until next morning, with a jeweller who had some fine lemon and smoky topazes well
set in silver, which Inge eventually succeeded in buying at not much
more than half his asking price. It was the last of our few days of real
idleness on the journey, and we enjoyed it, the four of us talking long
over our meals and drinks together. We had settled by now into the
kind of easy, good-humoured relationship in which shared discomforts
and pleasures open minds and natures to each other and deepen what
began as cordial acquaintance into real friendship.

The next day returned us to the familiar pattern of unexplained and
interminable delays too tedious for further detail: enough to say that
our plane to Bagdogra, which lies at the start of the mountain road to
Darjeeling, scheduled to leave at 11.35 a.m., left finally at 5.00 p.m.
The only breach in the agonizing boredom of those hours was the
landing of an immense Aeroflot transport plane on the runway in full
view of the lounge where we were waiting. Presumably it was carrying
some of the arms Russia has recently been supplying to India, but
nothing was immediately unloaded from it. What did happen, however,
was intriguing in its own way, for all at once we saw a new Rolls-
Royce – the only car of its kind we had yet seen in India – driving out

to the plane and, after a brief halt on the far side of the craft, returning the way it had come. Who or what had come from Russia so important as to merit such exalted transport? We had no plausible explanation, but an uneasy knowledge that the incident confirmed the closeness of Moscow to the Indian government of the day which, for all its historic opposition to colonialism and colonial wars, never had the moral courage to denounce effectively Russia's imperialist adventure in Afghanistan.

It was still light when we left Calcutta, but night was already falling in the shadow of the mountains when we reached Bagdogra, which lies at the foot of the Himalayas in a narrow corridor of Indian territory between Nepal and Bangladesh. From the air, we had seen the sun catching the peaks of the Himalayas, that last of our great Indian walls. Here, before we started on the mountain road, we had to register at an office where two army officers were taking the passports of foreigners, entering their names in a large book, and stamping permits. Darjeeling, like all the eastern foothills of the Himalayas, had been a restricted zone ever since the Chinese invasion of 1963, which scared the Indians into maintaining a strong military presence in the area and which may indeed be the real explanation for the Delhi government's consistent failure over the past twenty years to criticize Russian actions in Asia. Traditional Indian *realpolitik*, enunciated as early as the third century B.C. by King Chandragupta's minister Kautilya in his treatise on government called *Arthasastra*, has always proceeded on the maxim that "My enemy's enemy is my friend," without much Gandhian concern for the moral aspects of political situations. In Asian continental terms in the late twentieth century, this means an alignment with Russia against China, which has not only invaded India but has also committed the even worse sin in Indian eyes of befriending her most intimate enemy, Pakistan. And so, though it is by now a meaningless formality, foreigners have to stand in the queue at Bagdogra, whereas a resolute spy could easily escape from the ill-guarded airport in the jostling crowd of Indian passengers, of which no check was made.

Unless we took the bus to Siliguri some sixteen kilometres away and then caught the miniature train that snakes its way up the mountainsides – an exasperatingly slow procedure since it stops at every village and almost every tea plantation on the way – the only means of getting to Darjeeling was by car, and we hired one of the young Nepalis who were waiting beside their taxis outside the passport office to drive us there. He was a taciturn young man with an expressionless ivory-coloured face, but a good driver on the difficult mountain road. Inge and I had done this journey twice already, so that we could see in our mind's eyes the rain-forested mountain country, with its tea gardens and its Buddhist shrines, through which we were travelling in the dark. But for Toni and Yukiko, only the constant rising and twisting of the road and the flashes of tangled woodland caught in the headlights as we turned the corners told the kind of country through which we were steadily ascending. The people in the villages of wooden houses we passed through made it clear that we were entering a quite different cultural zone from the rest of India, however. They were either small and slender Nepalis, or even smaller Lepchas, or taller Tibetans with the robust chests of mountaineers, but all of them had a Mongolian cast to their features that clearly distinguished them from other people in India.

In ancient days this region was never part of India, and in historic times, until the British bought it from the ruler of Sikkim in 1835, Darjeeling – or Dorjeling, the place of the thunderbolt – was owned sometimes by the rulers of Sikkim and sometimes by the kings of Bhutan, but in either case was under the suzerainty of the Dalai Lama as the ruler of Tibet. The original inhabitants were the Lepchas, a tribal people whose animist altars are still to be seen beside the springs they worshipped. A ruling class of Tibetan nobles and lamas moved in to wield power over Sikkim and Bhutan, and turn them, if one can use so self-contradictory a term, into Buddhist theocracies, with the Redhat lamas of the Kargyupa sect in the ascendant. Under the British, large numbers of Nepalis moved in, for land and petty commerce; the Marwari merchants from Rajasthan came to share in the trade that flowed from Tibet through the nearby town of Kalimpong on the Bhutanese border, and Bengalis arrived as bureaucrats and clerks, a process that has accelerated since developments after independence made Darjeeling a part of the state of West Bengal.

A slow journey of ninety kilometres in the dark over winding mountain roads always seems as if it will never end, but at last we crossed the pass at Ghoom, 7,500 feet above sea level and ten kilometres out of Darjeeling, and began coasting down through drifts of cloud until we were in the upper streets of the town itself, aware of its steepness through the sweeping descents of lights below us. We had booked into an old British hotel, now run by Tibetans, of which Inge and I had good memories from our earlier visits there and the friendships we had then made. Most of those friends were now dead or departed: old

Sonam Thobten, the Sikkimese nobleman whose daughters we had befriended when they came to a Canadian university and who came to the hotel in 1964 in an orange brocade *chupa* (robe) carrying as a gift a beautiful old *thanka* which had been given him by the Panchen Lama, and followed by a servant with a basket of Himalayan tangerines on his head; Sister Vajra, an English lady turned Buddhist nun who was swept away in a landslide which destroyed the little house where we had visited her; and Yeshe Lhundug, a tall, ascetic Tibetan we found living in a slum house near the market, and who had been a high official of the Dalai Lama but fled the Summer Palace in Lhasa when the Chinese shelled it, swimming the river and making his way over the mountains to Bhutan; their names and their faces had come vividly back to me as we drove up through the mountains, but they were all gone.

The hotel lay on the crest of the high ridge up which the city climbs. In Darjeeling, as in most Indian hill stations, motor traffic is forbidden in the higher streets, which were used as pedestrian malls long before these became fashionable in North American and European cities, and we had to halt at the bottom of a steep footpath leading to the hotel and send a messenger to fetch the porters who loaded our luggage on their backs and, with tumplines around their brows, set off at a sharp pace up the path. It was a bitterly cold night in one of the worst Darjeeling winters in many years, and I set off after them with the idea of getting briskly warm, forgetting in how short a time we had come from sea level to more than seven thousand feet. The mountains laid their hands on me; I suddenly found myself gasping for air as I reached the courtyard outside the hotel, and had to collapse onto a bench as Toni hastily unpacked the McDowell's Premium to give me a quick swig. From that time on I remembered the rule of the mountains which I had learnt from suffering soroche (altitude sickness) in the high Andes: one step at a time taken slowly and you can go on for hours; speed up and you are incapacitated in a moment.

22. The Place of the Thunderbolt

Returning to the old hotel was a great mistake. We had never stayed there in such bitterly cold weather, nor had we reckoned with the decay which the intervening twelve years would have wrought. Nothing had been renewed in that decade; the curtains, the mattresses, the furniture, even the feeble old electric fires, were the same. Whatever heat the tiny fireplace emitted floated upward in the high-ceilinged rooms built for summer. A cough I had developed from the dust in Rajasthan came back with a vengeance and kept me awake all night; the cold activated Inge's dormant arthritis. By breakfast-time we were ready to take a car down to Bagdogra on the off-chance of getting a plane back to Delhi, but Toni and Yukiko persuaded us to try our luck at another hotel – new twelve years before – which we had dismissed as an example of the failure to transplant the western-style hotel into Asian countries. We remembered the indifferent staff and the execrable meals, compared with the fatherly servants and the good, solid food of the old hotel in those distant days.

But time, we discovered, had turned the tables, and not only metaphorically. The new hotel, indeed, had no guests at all, but the manager – a model of Indian courtesy – welcomed us as a happy omen for the coming season, and because we liked him, we decided to stay. We had no reason for regret. The rooms were low-ceilinged and snug, and by some miracle the kind of staff we remembered at the other hotel were now here: kindly old bearers who knew how to build a good coal fire and keep it going and, greatest treasure of all, a chef who had once served a European prince living in Kalimpong and whose crêpes suzettes and *pomfret amandine* were as superb as his curries and *gulab jaman*; never before had I encountered a cook who doubled so superbly in European and Indian cuisine. "This is your hotel," the manager would assure us each morning. "Order what you wish, and it shall be provided," as indeed it was.

There were two good reasons for us to come to Darjeeling: for Toni and Yukiko to experience another manifestation of the walls of India – this time the Buddhist shrines and temples in their appropriate setting of the great natural walls of the Himalayas; and for Inge and me to move again for a while among the Tibetans and other hill peoples to whom, in the past, we had devoted so much of our lives.

Darjeeling is a grandiose and rapidly decaying town in a setting of extraordinary natural beauty. What used to be the English part, the summer refuge of Calcutta officials and box wallahs in the days of the Raj, clings along the crests of a series of ridges whose slopes plunge downward on one side into the lower town where the Nepalis and Tibetans live around the noisy market, and on the other side into the greenery of tea plantations and racecourses, peasant hill farms and the dwindling remnants of mountainside forests, whose disappearance is the reason for the frequent landslides. Yet in the town itself, there are trees everywhere, thriving in the damp summer climate, deodars and tree rhododendrons lining the ridge crests and dotting the plunging slopes in among the big villas that are characteristic of Darjeeling and now, for the most part, are badly tended and decrepit from the battering of the monsoons. At times, especially in the very early mornings and late afternoons, when the mists move gently among the trees and the tragic-looking houses, the scene takes on a melancholy poignancy, as if the ghost of the Raj itself had risen up from the depths and stood in all its splendour and misery before one. Darjeeling owed its life to the British, and their departure has afflicted it like a lingering sickness.

The overbearing background to all of this is the vast, shining bulk of Kanchenjunga, at 28,208 feet less than a thousand feet lower than Everest and certainly as beautiful as its taller and more famous neighbour. Seeing Kanchenjunga is always a matter of luck. One can stay a week in Darjeeling and never see anything taller than the town's own ridges. But we were fortunate, and the pattern during our days there was a fairly reliable one. Early in the morning the veils would shift and the great glittering peaks and white ridges appear, rising out of their bed of dissolving clouds like a world forming out of chaos; with luck, the mountain would remain visible until noon, when the clouds would cover it until next morning.

Once again Toni showed an endurance in the cause of art that I found astonishing and impossible to imitate. Each day, while I was taking my first look at the mountain in the full morning sunlight before we went down to warm ourselves with the chef's excellent porridge, Toni would already have been picked up by a Nepali with a jeep and be driving up the rough roads to Tiger Hill, which lay a thousand feet above the pass at Ghoom, and was so much colder than the Darjeeling streets into which I would not be venturing for another hour. Rime would lie thick on the ground, and as Toni prepared his materials, the driver would forage over the hillside, picking up scraps of wood to build a fire behind his back that would give him at least a little warmth while he painted. When a painting was finished, Toni would light sheets of newspaper and wave them over it, so that the paint dried quickly and he could stow it away and move on to another equally exposed spot with a view over the mountain pastures and the cairn-like structures of the Tibetan *chötens*, or shrines, clustered under their waving lines of prayer flags.

Yukiko would not accompany Toni on these gruelling trips but would join Inge and me for breakfast and then await his return, while we would head for the lower town, in my particular concern for the detail of human life, or go wandering along the paths that cling to the summits of the hills and allow one to walk for miles outside Darjeeling, with fine views plunging down on every side.

When we went down to the market, it was by footpaths that linked the main streets and along which the poorer people lived. The houses were crowded and decrepit, yet the children who played around them were red-cheeked little mountaineers who greeted us with the laughter so characteristic of the Himalayan hill peoples. Eventually we would reach the station, to take a look at the little train with its blue carriages and its miniature steam engine whose tootings, echoing up the hill to the hotel, would wake us each morning as the first train set off for the plains at 7 a.m.

From the station we would walk along the lower streets where decrepitude became grime. Other Indian towns may be dirty, but it is usually in a sun-baked, dusty tropical way. The dirt that permeates the more crowded parts of Darjeeling is of a peculiarly northern kind like that of the industrial revolution towns of the English Midlands, and perhaps for the same cause, since Darjeeling is a cold place for several months of the year and, with the destruction of the forests in the Himalayan foothills by assiduous firewood gatherers, the sooty coal from Bihar has become the fuel generally used. But the grime was not only on the buildings. The hill peoples, and particularly those of Tibetan descent, do not share the Indian cult of personal cleanliness, and down in the market, the porters waited around, their clothes caked in dirt, their carrying robes on their shoulders, in the hope of an hour's employment. Some were boys no more than twelve years old, and two of these were fighting, so lost to everything except animosity that they lurched, fiercely grappling, into the path of a truck they had not even seen and only escaped being run over because some of the older porters dragged them out of its path.

Like all markets in modern Asia, that in Darjeeling was a mixture of the cosmopolitan and the traditional, with the traditional considerably less in evidence than on our first visit in the early 1960s. At that time, it was filled with refugees who had arrived there after the Dalai

Lama's flight in 1959 and had reinjected into the frontier town some of its earlier Tibetan character. Then, one saw hundreds of people dressed in traditional ways – not merely the monks in their maroon robes, but also laymen dressed in the belted gown or chupa, worn with high felt or leather boots and often with the wolfskin cap that distinguished the warrior herdsmen from Kham, who had fought most bitterly against the Chinese invaders. Then, the pavements of the market would be covered with artifacts the refugees had brought with them out of their world that history had just relegated to the past, and were selling for a little money to keep alive: jewellery, reliquaries studded with turquoise and coral, silver vessels, weapons, brocaded garments, thankas and block-printed books in the Tibetan script that was adapted from one of the early Indian alphabets.

The artifacts have long been absorbed into western collections without very much profit to their original owners, and the Tibetans, who still operate a good many of the stalls in the market, are no longer the exotic figures, their medieval splendour frayed by poverty, that they then appeared. The women still wear a muted version of their traditional garb of a chupa reaching to the heels and a striped apron if they are married, but the men all dress in the western manner and nobody walks along spinning a prayer wheel any more. But the gaunt faces of hunger that then haunted us have filled out, and there are no longer any Tibetan beggars. The Tibetans have found their places in a strange world, and as much by their own adaptability as through money given by foreigners or India's admirable tolerance for people from unfamiliar cultures.

This kind of combination and its excellent results were exemplified in the Tibetan Self-Help Centre outside Darjeeling, again, like Kabliji, one of those piecemeal efforts – Gandhi's "one step enough for me" – that transmit their messages of encouragement to those whose minds are paralysed by the enormity of India's problems. Inge and I set out for the Centre on a day when the wind was blowing cold off the snowy mountains. By the time we started, the mountains themselves were already veiled, but the lines of steep foothills receded into a blue haze toward Sikkim and the Tibetan border; below us, as we followed the mountain paths, the terraces of the tea gardens ran in precise curves around the contours of the lower slopes, and the gilded roof ornaments of the Bhutia Bastia Monastery shone in the sun above its brightly painted eaves. All the way along, on the terraces above and below the path, there were small houses, mostly of planks, with little structures of wood and string on the roofs that are called ghost traps and are meant to ward off malign influences. The children played outside, the women knitted or sewed in the sunlight and greeted us as we passed in singsong English, and often there was a cat playing or asleep and always well fed, for the Tibetans are so attached to these animals that they have a saying: "It is better to desecrate seven temples than to kill a cat!"

It was a good hour and a half's walk to the Centre, which occupied a promontory jutting out from the main ridge; its buildings spilt in a series of terraces down the hillside and centred on a kind of square surrounded by workshops on one of the larger benches. As we descended the steps past the little *gompa*, or temple, we saw a small, familiar figure in trim chupa and apron, talking with authoritative gestures, and hurried down to receive her surprised greeting. She was Mrs Thondup, wife of Gyalo Thondup, the Dalai Lama's elder brother. A Chinese woman who made the Tibetans' cause her own, she has worked tirelessly for the refugees, yet still maintains a kind of personal aloofness so that nobody seems to know her first name; I have known her nearly a quarter of a century, always as Mrs Thondup. She had founded the Self-Help Centre in 1960, as a way of using Tibetan skills to provide the economic basis of a new life for the refugees in what she anticipated – and events were to prove – would be a long exile.

In a traditional situation where large numbers of men, including many of the most able, retreated into the great monasteries, Tibetan women gained considerable power and influence. Among the common people, they carried on much of the trading; among the aristocracy, they wielded great power in the noble houses that shared the administration of the country with the monkish bureaucrats. There was even, in the religious sphere, an abbess, bearing the strange name of Thunderbolt Sow (Dorje Phagmo), who ranked among the five great incarnations of Tibet, perhaps not the equal of the Dalai Lama or the Panchen Lama, but certainly on the same level of sanctity as the Sakya Lama and Karmapa, the head of the Kargyupa sect.

When the Dalai Lama fled from Lhasa in 1959, with many of the noblemen and high ecclesiastics, as well as large numbers of ordinary people who resented the destruction of their religion by the invading Chinese, the administration he created fell into two categories. The noblemen formed a kind of government in exile centred on the *kashag* (or cabinet), and wielded what were largely phantom powers, since, though they had people to represent, they had no land to govern. But the real task was keeping the refugees alive, and developing a new

economic basis for their existence in India, and here the powerful women
of Lhasa emerged among the dominant figures. There was Rinchen
Dolma Taring, whose husband, Jigme Taring, belonged to the royal
line of Sikkim and who established a big settlement for refugee children
and old people at Mussoorie in the central foothills above Dehra Dun,
based on the Pestalozzi villages of Switzerland. It was taken over later
by our friend Khando Yapshi, the Dalai Lama's niece. There was Tser-
ing Dolma, the Dalai Lama's older sister, who set up another children's
settlement at Dharamsala in the west, near the Kashmir border, which
was taken over after her death by His Holiness's younger sister, Padma
Gyalpo. And there was Mrs Thondup away to the east at Darjeeling,
basing her approach on sustaining the family through work. We have
enjoyed the friendship of all of them, women of energy and intelligence,
the fine products of a society where the feminine role has traditionally
been an active one; Mrs Thondup exemplified the kind of forceful
personality that fitted admirably into such a world.

Her energy seemed undiminished as she demonstrated how the
Centre had grown since we walked into its first rough shacks so many
years before. Four hundred workers and their families were now supported and, together with orphans and old people to whom the Centre
gave a home, they represented a good proportion of the ten thousand
Tibetans still living in and around Darjeeling.

As we went from one workshop to another, we realized not merely
how versatile the Centre had become in its continuation of the traditions
of Tibetan craftsmanship, but also how it had become integrated into
a self-sufficient community, rather like a great joint family. Carpet
weaving was the leading industry. The process began with the carding
and spinning of Tibetan wool brought in from Nepal on treadle machines using old bicycle wheels. The old women played a leading role
here, and the spinning shed was the one place where we still heard the
low, monotonous drone of chanted prayers, which the younger people
no longer practise; some of the women were in their nineties, with
shrivelled, toothless faces, but in the tradition of Asian joint families
they preferred to keep on making their contribution – however small
– to the communal economy rather than enduring the tedium of illiterate
idleness. (The oldest inhabitant of the Centre was a man of 102, and
even he had a task, to look after the kennel of apsos – Lhasa terriers –
that the Centre reared.) Next came the dyeing sheds where the wool
was dipped in great iron vats, some of them containing vegetable dyes
made from the piles of leaves and branches that were stored there, and

others containing chemical dyes; the vegetable-dyed carpets were woven for export to foreign collectors who preferred the more muted traditional colours, and the gaudy chemical-dyed ones were mostly bought by Indians who visited the Centre. In the weaving sheds, the bird-like chatter and laughter of the younger women was punctuated by the clatter of the handmade wooden carpet looms. On smaller looms, other women were weaving cotton and woollen materials to make aprons and shoulder bags, and the oldest weavers used primitive backstrap looms to make bright-coloured belts.

The men had their own workshops, fabricating wooden tables and chests that were carved and richly painted and gilded in traditional Tibetan designs, and carving demon masks for use in sacred dances; the joiners also made looms and Gandhian spinning wheels for use in the Centre, and window frames and doors to be used in the new housing which masons belonging to the community were putting up on the hillside. In the painters' studio, old artists were teaching their apprentices the meticulous techniques of Tibetan sacred scroll painting, and in the metal workshops, smiths were creating silver ceremonial vessels, and rings set with turquoise and local amethyst, and copper inkpots. A store in the square sold the products of the various workshops, and the tea grown in neighbouring plantations, to casual visitors, and carpets were being packed there for export to Zurich and London, to Hamburg and New York. Another store was the cooperative, where the workers in the Centre could buy necessities a little more cheaply than in the town. There was even a dairy, with its own herd of eighteen cows to provide milk for children and invalids.

Clearly, it was economic need and economic success that held together this community based on a fortunate conjunction of supply and demand: the Tibetans' retained ability to practise their traditional crafts, and a wide market for artifacts recalling a vanished society far in the mountains that still holds an especially romantic place in the contemporary imagination. But when we looked at other aspects of the Centre it was clear that a great deal more in the way of social imagination had gone into it. The school, with its 350 children, was closed for the winter holidays, but in some of its rooms young people now receiving higher education at St Joseph's College in Darjeeling – which is largely run by Canadian Jesuits and which has evolved, since I have known it, from an imitation English public school into a university – were devoting their own vacation to training the more backward children. The feeling of a living community in which each generation, from the children up to the old people, played its appropriate role, was very strong here.

Yet the sense of mutual responsibility of which we became so strongly aware was not restricted to the Centre, as we realized when Mrs Thondup took us down to the whitewashed little wooden hospital and introduced us to Dr Wangyi, one of the first Tibetans to take western medical training. The hospital was open not only to the workers at the Centre and their families, but also to other Tibetans living in this part of Darjeeling and to the workers in the neighbouring tea gardens, who were mostly tribal people with no medical services of their own; people sometimes came seeking treatment from as far away as Sikkim, and Dr Wangyi would make regular visits to the tea gardens to check on sick people and sanitary arrangements. Like the Kabliji Hospital, the Tibetan Self-Help Centre was not a hermetically sealed unit; it was reaching outward, now that its own people were provided for, seeking new outlets for its help.

As Inge and I walked back along the hill paths, and talked of the Centre and of Kabliji and of the schemes for helping tribal peoples that Davinson and Fernandez had outlined in Bangalore, it became clearer to us that there might never be a great overriding politicians' solution for India's ills, but that the proliferation of such limited efforts, keeping alive the true spirit of Gandhism, must in the end bring changes for the better. As so often during the years that we have been involved in such ventures, I found Auden's great verse echoing in my mind like a prayer:

> Defenceless under the night
> Our world in stupor lies;
> Yet, dotted everywhere,
> Ironic points of light
> Flash out wherever the Just
> Exchange their messages;
> May I, composed like them
> Of Eros and of dust,
> Beleagured by the same
> Negation and despair
> Show an affirming flame.

As evening came on, Darjeeling underwent a strange transformation. The mists formed in small woolly clouds on the hillside and moved like amorphous beings among the trees; in the last light, the blue smoke of the evening fires began to hover, the fuzzy twinkling of street lights glowed, and the atmospheric magic of the Indian hills swept over the scene, washing out from one's sight and mind all the decrepitude and filth that in the daylight made such a depressing contrast with memories of a more splendid past. Wandering along the high lanes at this hour, we would pass little stalls lit by flickering candles, and doors in plank houses open onto tiny rooms where there were books on shelves and children writing; other children shouted and played tipcat in the road, and young women greeted us in soft Nepali voices as they passed in the dusk. They were moments of affecting human joy and gentleness, when the decay of a city seemed as irrelevant as the splendid indifference of the now invisible mountain walls.

23. Spring Climbs the Mountains

Darjeeling had given us India's most visibly lofty walls in the great ranges of the Himalayas and their foothills, not to mention the smaller, less physical walls that divided the peoples of its polyglot society. Now it was time to return to Delhi, which had always been the pivot of our Indian travels.

The plane was due to leave Bagdogra in the mid-afternoon, and at noon we started out from the hotel, down the long, narrow, winding road to the plains, the same road we had taken a few days before in the darkness. In daylight it was a splendidly scenic journey: ten kilometres climbing along the edges of a deep green valley to the pass at Ghoom and the last flashing glimpse of Kanchenjunga just before the clouds immersed its topmost pinnacles, and then seventy kilometres driving down through the foothills from nearly eight thousand feet to almost sea level, with endlessly changing vistas of high ridges and deeply descending valleys, all covered with rainforest except where the hillsides had been shaved for tea plantations. It was a journey also through the seasons, for at the pass there were only hardy little daisies blooming, but as we descended, more and brighter flowers appeared: great drifts of golden coreopsis and a blue plant resembling heliotrope and, just below the halfway village of Kurseong, blossoming almonds that heralded the start of spring's climb back up the mountainside.

It is hard anywhere in India to escape the sense that one is among a people whose religion is still active, but nowhere did we feel this so strongly as in these northern hills, where religious buildings of one kind or another were not only numerous but quite obviously actively used. We passed several temples of Tibetan Buddhists, their façades brilliantly – almost gaudily – painted and their roofs carrying gilded finials and sculptures of Buddha's wheel supported by its attendant deer. Everywhere, standing in little groups on hillsides, were the white-painted *chötens* planted there by dedicated people to gain merit and perhaps a better rebirth after death. At Ghoom there was a Lepcha shrine with conventionalized dog-like lion figures, and farther down, these animists had erected little structures of branches and banana plants to placate the spirits at some of the hillside springs. In some places, there were lines of simple Muslim gravestones.

But Hinduism was equally in evidence, for it is the religion of most Nepalis, who become more numerous in the lower ranges of the foot-hills, and all along the way they were erecting arches of coniferous boughs and hanging lines of little coloured pennants for the festival of Saraswati, the goddess of learning and music, who is especially revered in this region. Outside a cluster of houses we saw one of the images of the goddess made especially for the festival, clad in a purple robe with gold stars and holding a sitar made of gilded cardboard and tinsel; she was awaiting the procession in two days' time when she would be taken out with great music and chanting and in a final ceremony be dipped into a sacred tank whose waters would dissolve her body of unbaked clay. The gods too, this lesson seems to teach, are mortal, caught in the great cycles of endlessly repeated time. But Saraswati is also, among other roles, the deity of writing in the Hindu pantheon, and as a writer, I always wonder at the significance of this annual dissolution of my patron goddess. Is it that individual works are as ephemeral as Saraswati's clay figure, but the great images always return?

At last the road levelled out into the plains and suddenly, after the long stretches when we would have the mountain road to ourselves, driving through forests of teak and bamboo that were silent except for the call of birds, the country became crowded. It was the real Bengal, a different world from the peripheral Bengal of the mountain peoples, and the folk too, in their dhotis and turbans and shirts hanging loose over duck trousers, with their darker, sharper features and narrower chests, were different. Villages were numerous, two at least always in sight at the same time, and the dwellings were once again the insub-stantial structures of a hot climate; we passed through one potters' settlement where the big round vessels of red clay they made were piled up among houses made of the cane that grows by all the local rivers: nothing but cane in the whole place so that even the temple was the same kind of fragile structure as the houses, and recognizable only by the religious flags flying from its roof peak. The roads were dense with people and cows walking, and with buses packed to the doors with people who also sat on the roofs and clung like strange fruit to the back and the sides.

We reached Bagdogra, reported to the military authorities to have our departure recorded in their great book, and checked in at the airport. We waited for the plane, an hour, two hours, and then Indian Airlines played its last and worst trick on us. There would, its manager an-nounced, be no plane at all to Delhi today; we might expect to fly out at noon tomorrow. The local passengers were sent home; the rest of us were bundled into a bus and taken to a new hotel on the outskirts of Siliguri, one of those bleak, institutional concrete structures that are gradually replacing the spacious old hotels of the Raj. There was nothing to do, since we were several miles out of the town and Siliguri is, in any case, one of the dullest country towns in India. Toni did not feel the urge to paint; the flat landscape offered not a flicker of inspiration. I sat and wrote in my diary the depressed thoughts that come in times of frustration at the end of tiring journeys: the thoughts one keeps out of the final narrative lest one's readers assume that travel is a universally tedious occupation; I read, for consolation, *Oblomov*.

There was a time, late the following morning, when I wondered if we would even get out of Bagdogra on the second day, for we hung about the hotel listening to the biographies of our fellow passengers and waiting for the bus until after noon; when we got to the airport there was no sign of a plane, and to pacify us, a lunch of fish cooked rather well in the Bengali way, with mustard oil, was provided. This struck me as an ominous sign. But eventually the craft appeared, a special rescue flight; we left Bagdogra at 2.30 p.m., stopped at Patna on the way, and got into Delhi three hours later – but more than twenty-nine hours after we had left Darjeeling on a journey that should have taken us, at most, seven hours. It was the last time, I resolved, that I would ever travel by air in India.

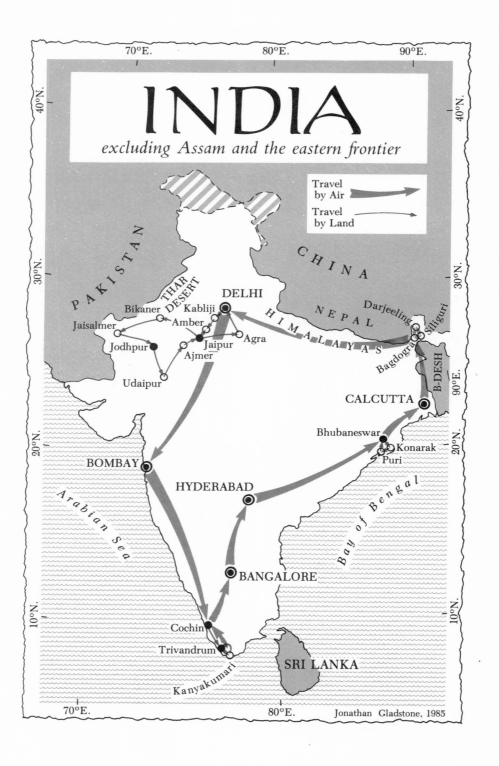

INDIA

excluding Assam and the eastern frontier

Travel by Air
Travel by Land

CHINA

PAKISTAN

THAR DESERT

Bikaner   Kabliji
Jaisalmer   Amber
    Jodhpur   Jaipur   Agra
        Ajmer
    Udaipur

DELHI

NEPAL   Darjeeling

HIMALAYAS   Siliguri
        Bagdogra
            B-DESH

CALCUTTA

Bhubaneswar
    Konarak
    Puri

Arabian Sea

BOMBAY

HYDERABAD

Bay of Bengal

BANGALORE

Cochin
Trivandrum

Kanyakumari

SRI LANKA

Jonathan Gladstone, 1985

VI

EPILOGUE: DELHI

24. The City of Conquerors

Delhi is the most un-Indian city of India, a conqueror's capital, with all the splendour and strangeness such a description implies; it has never completely shed the influences that percolate from the long period of almost seven hundred years when it was the centre from which successive invading Muslim dynasties ruled India, creating in the process no fewer than seven distinct cities scattered over the considerable area of the Jumna valley which Delhi now occupies. The walls of their fortified citadels, like Sher Shah's sixteenth-century Purana Qila, their solidly built monuments, like the austerely beautiful Lodi Tombs in New Delhi, and their castle palaces, like Shah Jehan's Red Fort in Old Delhi, are unavoidable components of one's visual impression of the city, with a Muslim ruin at the end of almost every vista. The great frame in which they are seen is the master plan the British created when they, too, were drawn to this seat of the conquerors, and in 1912 moved the capital of the Raj from Calcutta and built a New Delhi that would outshine all the Delhis of the past.

This is the Delhi of which any visitor is likely to be most conscious. Unless he is willing to accept the penalty of long taxi drives by choosing the charming old British hostelry, Maidens, in Old Delhi, he is likely to stay in a hotel on one of the leafy avenues of the new city. He will do most of his shopping in Janpath and in thoroughfares like Connaught Circus and Connaught Place, where the names of the conquerors still linger, and if he is intent on travelling to other parts of India, it is there that he will have to go through the slow and exasperatingly chit-ridden process of making his travel arrangements.

Living in Delhi gives one an immediately untypical impression of India, largely because the crowds who make Delhi the subcontinent's third largest community live in the narrow streets of Shah Jehan's old city around the Red Fort and the Jama Masjid. New Delhi is mainly a city for the privileged and their servants into which the workers in the government offices pour each morning in a flood of bicycles and buses.

Apart from heavily used streets like Janpath, its avenues and circles bear a slight burden of traffic and retain, to an astonishing extent, the feeling of the peaceful garden city that Sir Edwin Lutyens planned; indeed, it is because of its openness, as distinct from the congestion of more typical north Indian cities like Agra and Benares and Calcutta, that Delhi does to an extent resemble the loosely planned cities of South India like Bangalore and Trivandrum and even Madras. Our companions, on first arrival there, were astonished at the quietness, the sense of leisure, and when we got to Jaipur, with its noise and smell and packed traffic, Toni had remarked to me, "Now this is what I thought Delhi would be like!"

Government is the main function of New Delhi. Bombay and Calcutta are still the business centres of the country, and also the places where the arts, including the great Indian film industry, flourish. In all the years since I have known Delhi, I have encountered interesting writers there only when some special occasion attracted them, like the great Tagore celebration of 1961 at which, on my first visit to India, I met more poets and novelists than I have ever encountered in Delhi since.

The kind of world one dips into on reaching Delhi is in fact very much like that which greets the visitor to Ottawa, a little more exotic because of the setting, but essentially as alien to – and as parasitic on – the real life of the country. There are the diplomats, a dull lot since Octavio Paz ceased to be Mexico's Ambassador and James George to be Canada's High Commissioner; most western countries convey an implied slight to India's pretensions by their choice of second-raters to represent them, and no diplomat who can pick Paris or Rome or the United Nations is likely to plump for Delhi. Surprisingly few politicians move through the social circles of the city, which tend to be dominated by the high civil servants, the successors to the Indian Civil Service of the British, who have inherited from the Raj a contempt for the elected representatives of the people. Such bureaucrats tend to be highly educated men with a touch of cosmopolitan – or at least Oxbridge – polish, and they would talk well on almost every subject except politics, which at the time of our visit was taboo at Delhi social occasions; largely because it is a city of tale-bearers. Those who could not speak well of Mrs Gandhi's government, which was probably the case with most highly placed public servants, were not willing to risk her noted vengefulness by speaking against her in company. The memory of the Emergency years, when she indiscriminately imprisoned her opponents and critics – from the revered Jayaprakash Narayan to the witty and beautiful Maharani of Jaipur – was not lost, nor was it forgotten that when the late prime minister had to defend her power, she resorted to old regulations that had first been formulated by the British viceroys for dealing with Indian Nationalists.

If a word of dissent did emerge on such occasions, it was likely to come from the chorus of second-rate writers and painters and journalists who seek their fortunes in the shadow of power, charming people often, but by no means the best their country can offer. Like Ottawa again, Delhi is the kind of place where mediocrities, from lack of the competition of first-rate minds, can cultivate their substantial *amours propres*.

This world, we realized all the more clearly when we returned to Delhi for the last time, had very little to do – except for the inconvenient fact that it ruled it – with the India of desert cities and provincial towns and southern and eastern villages through which we had been travelling for the past two months. Again, as on all my previous visits to the capital, I saw eyes shifting in incomprehension or glazing in lack of interest when I talked of what we had seen in Kerala and Orissa and remoter Rajasthan. Indeed, the only man with whom I had intelligent conversations on rural India during our last days in Delhi was the former ruler·of a little state in the Kulu valley near Kashmir who fitted uncomfortably into the Delhi environment because his sympathies were all with rustic people whose fates held little interest for the place-seekers in this city of conquerors.

Delhi is still, though the actors have changed, the city of Empire, the city of power. A couple of days before we finally left for Burma, Inge and I had to go from Claridge's Hotel, where we were staying, to Connaught Place in the city centre. Normally the way was a very direct one, along Aurangzeb Road to the bottom of Janpath, and then straight up to the Place, with the National Museum on our right, and on our left the long vistas of Rajpath, "the way of kings," terminated by the hybrid roofs and towers of the Rashtrapati Bhavan, the former viceroy's residence which is now the president's palace. This time, however, we had hardly left the hotel before we began to be diverted by a series of police barriers that took us out of our way through the Mogul gardens of the palace.

I had been at the palace once, at a reception in the great audience hall, with turbaned red-coated lancers on guard and gold-braided musicians in the marble gallery as the president, then the philosopher Radakrishnan, walked among the guests, but I had never had the kind of leisurely look which the slow progress of Delhi traffic through these back ways gave us at the exterior of the building. In design, as well as in its red stone, Lutyens' masterpiece perpetuated in Indian terms the tradition of imperial power, for it was largely modelled on the beautiful and tragic city of Fatehpur Sikri that Akbar built in 1569 and inexplicably deserted in 1588, as we recognized from having revisited the place a month before on our way from Jaipur to Delhi. But at one point, turning a corner, we saw an echo of an earlier imperialism, that of Ashoka, in the foreparts of an elephant that seemed to be emerging from a wall beside an archway, a distant recollection of that elephant stepping out of the virgin rock that we had seen in the hills above Bhubaneswar.

In building the great new city that was completed in 1930 – only seventeen years before they handed it over to a free India – the British were consciously, in the last flamboyant phase of the Raj, equating the rule of the King Emperor with the rule of the ancient Hindu-Buddhist Chakravartins and of the Moguls who were the contemporaries of the Tudors and Stuarts; because their control over India had become even more complete than that of either Ashoka or Akbar, they intended to build the greatest of all the imperial cities. Though, as men of commerce, the East India Company ruled from Calcutta on its great tidal river, Delhi had always fascinated them, in the way it still fascinates the Indians, as a locus of power. In 1857, at the outbreak of the Mutiny, the last of the Moguls, Bahadur Shah, still reigned as titular emperor in Delhi, and it was his symbolic importance as well as that of the city and its Red Fort that led the mutineers of the Meerut garrison to ride there immediately, massacre the British, and get control of the aged, opium-sodden survivor of the last imperial dynasty, whom they immediately made their puppet leader. The British alike recognized the importance of taking control of this ancient centre of power, and the recapture of Delhi was their first objective in countering the Mutiny; it was attained five days before Havelock fought his way into Lucknow. Two historic institutions then came to an end almost simultaneously. The last of the Moguls was formally deposed and the administration of the country was taken out of the hands of the East India Company, which had been dabbling in the affairs of the subcontinent for two and a half centuries.

An English queen became the Empress of India and the British Raj began its ninety-year career. At first the Raj still governed, as the East India Company had done, from Calcutta, but the new rulers were uneasy in that trading city and the glamour of Delhi's history fascinated them, so it was in Delhi in 1903 that Lord Curzon received the homage of the native princes in an atmosphere of imperial pomp at his great durbar, and in 1911 that King George V, the first reigning monarch to visit India, held the durbar at which he announced the transfer of the capital. The following year Lord Hardinge arrived in vice-regal procession, mounted on an elephant, to lay the foundation stone of the eighth Delhi, and was wounded by a bomb thrown by a terrorist of nationalist sympathies.

The British have gone, but power and its pomp are still nurtured in Delhi, where the president of a country liberated largely by Gandhi's austere non-violent methods, and by a philosophy that negated political power, lives protected by a flamboyantly uniformed Bodyguard that originally watched over the viceroy in the palace built for the proconsul of an alien and conquering power.

We returned by another route from Connaught Place, and then we saw that the great diversions of traffic were due to preparations being made in the Rajpath for the processions on Republic Day, a few days after our departure, and soon we passed the parks where soldiers and equipment were being assembled to rehearse the parade. The martial races the British had recruited – Sikhs and Rajputs and Gurkhas and Jats – were all there in their distinctive uniforms and, even more characteristic of the power orientation of the occasion, there were the lines of new tanks and guns and missile carriers.

They were, indeed, the troops and weapons of an independent India rather than those of a conquering alien empire, but the kind of power they exemplified was the same as that of the Raj, the power of physical force and ultimately death, and nothing could have seemed more antithetical to the spirit of Gandhi's non-violent disobedience as a means of social struggle. The choice of Delhi as the capital was a manifestation of Nehru's rejection of Gandhi's example and arguments as a guiding philosophy for the new India. A Gandhian India, negating power as well as violence and basing itself on traditional village culture rather than on the cities created by foreign conquerors (whether Delhi or Bombay, Calcutta or Madras), would not have chosen as its centre the place that, since the defeat of its Rajput king Prithviraja eight hundred years ago, has always been the seat of power wielded by alien conquerors.

There seems a fatal connection between the spirit of a place and the actions of those who inhabit it, and undoubtedly the governments that have ruled in Delhi since 1947 have been influenced in many ways by the imperial *genius loci*. They became detached from the villagers, that salt of India which Gandhi cherished, and this meant that they were losing contact with three quarters of their country's population. They gave way to the temptation of military ventures to ensure territory, invading in turn Hyderabad and Kashmir and Goa. They sought the easy way out through industrialization, and their consequent neglect of the rural areas meant that urban problems became ever more acute because millions of people whom the countryside could not provide with work and a living swelled the great and desperate slums outside the cities, the infamous bustees. Liberated from Britain, India still remained a kind of empire, governed by native-born sahibs, with the cities ruling and plundering the villages and the rich ruling and plundering the poor.

Perhaps the greatest of all the walls of which we became aware in India were not those of buildings and mountains, nor yet the less visible walls of caste and language and religious community, strong though these remain, but the great walls that have been erected in Delhi – that agglomeration of imperial capitals – between the rulers' symbolic conception of India's grandeur and the real misery experienced by the people. The annual military parade, for which we had just seen preparations, was one example. An even more dramatic one was that of the Asian games held in the city during 1982 which became the occasion for building many new structures that dwarfed most of the conquerors' monuments that Toni spent his time painting, in all the beauty that age and irrelevance had given them.

According to fairly reliable estimates, a total of about 500 million dollars was spent from public and private sources on the games: building stadia, athletes' villages, overpasses, road widenings and a mass of new hotels, which were not filled because the expected crowds did not arrive from abroad. This occasion brought no benefit to India except a little prestige among the non-aligned countries. But it consumed vast amounts of money in Indian terms on a non-productive venture in a year when several thousand people died of famine in Bihar, when bustee dwellers near the sites of the games had still to make do with one water tap for a hundred or more shacks, when literally hundreds of millions of Indians had neither pure water nor enough to eat. Such a flamboyant attempt to enhance the national image merely emphasized the height of the walls that in India divide those two nations whom Disraeli, talking of nineteenth-century England, defined as "the Privileged and the People."

Everywhere in India we heard anxious people remarking that "the rich are getting richer and the poor, poorer," and though there were no statistics to prove the truth or falsehood of such a statement, the social commentators seem to be agreed that out of India's population, currently approaching 700 million, around 300 million are at a level of destitution far below the poverty line accepted in western countries, with no land, no housing better than shacks, no jobs worth the name, no prospects. At the same time, in the protective shadow of the military industrial state, a numerous middle class has arisen whose conspicuous spending is exemplified in the big, new suburbs of expensive villas that have appeared in areas around Delhi, where in past years was only scrubland inhabited by snakes and partridges. This class shows all the callousness and vulgarity that in every time and place have been characteristics of the *nouveau riche*, reinforced by a belief, not unlike that held by certain materialistic Calvinists, that some men are predestined by their karma to be rich and most to be poor. Most of the politicians of modern India are either too much a part of the rising middle class to care about the poor, or too fatalistic to believe that any dramatic change in the Indian social structure is likely or even possible.

And they are perhaps correct, in the sense that efforts following on the orientation of Indian governments toward seeking solutions in industrialization and urbanization are bound to have little success. A truer way for a country so rural in the heart of its being was Gandhi's plan for a decentralized society based on the revivification of the villages. But this was the plan that Nehru rejected when he set about creating a nation-state in the western style centred on Delhi, the city of the conquerors, at the same time as he rejected, in the moment of independence, Gandhi's warning that "the militarization of India would mean self-destruction." What a supreme mockery that Gandhi was given a military funeral and, on the spot beside the Jumna where his fragile body was burnt, an elaborate monument he would in life have disdained! It was in Delhi that the evil forces came together that would kill Gandhi. One cannot imagine in that locus of power a real home for the spirit of the man who said that "self-government means continuous effort to be free of governmental control, whether it is foreign or national," and that "the ideally non-violent state will be an ordered anarchy."

At the end of this journey over the winter of 1982–3, I became more than ever convinced that India has given the world three of its greatest moral beings, an extraordinary record for any nation: Buddha and Ashoka and Gandhi. But the Buddha's message has been so dis-